LETTERS TO THE EDITOR

Apostle Terrence P. Honoré

LETTERS TO THE EDITOR

Copyright © 2022 Apostle Terrence P. Honoré.

All rights reserved. No part of this book may be used or reproduced by any means, graphic, electronic, or mechanical, including photocopying, recording, taping or by any information storage retrieval system without the written permission of the author except in the case of brief quotations embodied in critical articles and reviews.

Because of the dynamic nature of the Internet, any web addresses or links contained in this book may have changed since publication and may no longer be valid. The views expressed in this work are solely those of the author and do not necessarily reflect the views of the publisher, and the publisher hereby disclaims any responsibility for them.

ISBN: 978-9-7682-9004-5 (sc)

Print information available on the last page.

LETTERS

TO

THE

EDITOR

DEDICATION

To my dear wife Judith David Honoré,

for the many years of caring and sharing the challenges

of life. The many moments when we pondered on the

things that were happening around us, and all the

experiences that life brought our way.

We thank God.

ENDORSEMENTS

The old adage of "Being too heavenly for any earthly good" could not be applied to Apostle Terrence Honore who has distinguished himself among his peers as someone who has a passion for God and an unshakable belief in Jesus Christ his Son; to a total reliance on the Holy Spirit on whom he depends on for wisdom and guidance.

His interests are many and varied and he has not been afraid to tackle issues that are topical and has always been willing to speak on behalf of the Church. Topics like ethics, politics, health, wellness, holistic development, and education are but a few of the topics that this ecumenist has been able to address the editor on our behalf.

This publication will make for good reading as readers will be able to have the articles in book form. Happy Reading!!

Reverend Duane Samm Methodist Minister (Superintendent)

Apostle Terrance Honore, a minister of religion, historian, communications professional, and community activist, demonstrates his commitment to nation-building and positively impacting lives in this compilation of letters published in the country's daily newspapers.

In these op-ed pieces, he provides a strong Christian perspective on a range of issues affecting Trinidad and Tobago. They encompass a quarter-century of political, social, and cultural issues which, viewed in chronological order, provide some insight and solutions to the challenges of this modern, post-Independence nation that are as relevant now as they were when first written.

Suzanne Sheppard

Professional Journalist/ Lead Editor, Newsgathering Trinidad Guardian

The book comprises a series of letters to the editor of one of our daily newspapers over a period extending over twenty years. It demonstrates clearly and unequivocally, the "real life" that has become so often the bone of our society. It also highlights as well, many of the things that we can, by the Grace of God, achieve in this life and enjoy what we believe and further pray "And may God bless our nation".

The narrative that develops out of this collection of 'Letters' to the Editor, calls for a proclamation from the heart, a yearning and a longing for the best that can emerge, not merely 'the best of us" but from "all of us" with a mighty exultation of the wonderful words of life.

Noted hymn writer P. P. Bliss penned a wonderful song of praise about one hundred years ago that exalts in totality "The Wonderful Words of Life":

"Let me more of their beauty see,

Wonderful words of Life, Words of Life and beauty

Teach me Faith and Duty

Beautiful Words, Wonderful Words of Life"

A song, I believe that has disappeared from our hearts and our lives. This book engagingly written by Rev Terrence Honore' brings to our attention many of the things that deprive and rob us of this heritage of life i.e., that of life that is ours to enjoy, live out, and further fulfil in varied ways – revealing our humanity, and the spark of divinity that resides in each and every one of us.

There are many quotes that jump out to you as you read this book, and many observations, comments, and wry bits of humour. The letters are updates, like the headlines of today, whether on radio, newspaper, television, or even from the lips of our friends, neighbours, or even our enemies.

I commend to you the reader to read this volume carefully and thoughtfully, then do not store it away in your bookshelf/study–already bulging with many a book – but do this, lend, pass it on to a fellow worker or friend, to a sister or brother, or even a stranger with a quiet prayer. Amen.

Rev Ken Kalloo
Presbyterian Minister and Archivist of the Church

TABLE OF CONTENTS

Dedication v

Endorsements vii

Foreword xv

Author's Preface xvii

Acknowledgements xix

Introduction xxi

Minshall has crossed the line 1

Call for Christians to declare war on crime 3

Don't Suffer Little children 5

Crime is a Spiritual Thing 8

Let the Church arise! 12

Deliver us from Freeport Evil 17

Time for a Christian manifesto 21

Palmiste... preserve the history 24

Wisdom for our problems 27

Endemic problem of epidemic proportions.. 28

Whither the widows 31

Without South, there can be no North 33

The country 'ayo', don't let treasury go too 35

Rough weather on sea and land for TT 37

The Church needs to do more for the poor and ill 39

Call Day of Prayer and Thanksgiving, Mr PM 42

Turn to prayer to arrest crime 44

Time to have place for the steelpan... 47

Roundabout nation that's T&T 50

'Botanic gardens' in south needs care 53

Requiem for the Gulf of Paria? 56

Mob pursuit of the CJ just will not do 59

Country needs a purge, Mr PM 61

Scholars must do right for God and country 64

Let's celebrate unity of TT 67

Praise For Police Action 70

A highway for Hasely 72

Time to go to church 74

Let's care for the caregivers 77

Christmas is for Christians 79

South churches ready to support laid-off workers 82

Stay up, Mr Commissioner 84

Christians and Carnival 87

Let's respect our holy days 91

Do away with SEA sin 94

Let's stand with the men in blue 96

Baring the truth 99

Please, no lies as you eulogize 102

Palmiste... preserve the history 104

Keeping time in San Fernando 107

Let's fix the flooding 110

Columbus was seen in Sando 112

A symbol for Sando 115

Better roads ahead in 2020 117

Prayer is essential 120

Sando Library.... red and ready to be restored 122

'Politicitis' Alert! 125

Make National Day of Prayer permanent 128

More bacchanal with cancelling of Carnival 130

Let's keep Sunday sacred...133

Defeating our post-covid19 demons... 136

Lead on, Minister Cox 139

Stop the 'acting' for top cop..142

Promises spoken, promises broken. 146

Shuffling the Political Deck 149

Time to clean out the War Bunkers!! 152

Faith in farming 155

Time to test the talk 159

Democracy in Distress...163

Stop Hating our Heritage 167

Apostle Terrence Honoré 170

FOREWORD

LETTERS TO THE EDITOR

This book consists of several letters to two national newspapers in Trinidad and Tobago written over a period of twenty-five years. The letters address a wide variety of topics that affected community and national life.

The book treats issues faced by the church and nation and offers sound solutions. For instance, he deals with matters such as how Christians should be proactive in working to minimize crime, the need to protect the vulnerable children of our nation, calls for a carnival band-man to respect sacred things, addresses faulty road engineering on a highway that may have contributed to high road fatalities in two sections of the roadway, and several other matters.

The writer, Apostle Terrence Honoré, is informed, skilled and an advocate for national development. He is a historian and journalist by training. He courageously and simultaneously interacts with issues that many church leaders only address in the pulpit. His worldview is unapologetically Christian.

Apostle Honoré has a wide experience from the private sector, public sector, the wider church community, and the sporting fraternity which is skilfully interwoven into the book.

As a person who has served over three decades in tertiary theological education and about twenty-five years in the pastoral, I recommend this book to church leaders, Christians in general, and the citizens of Caricom nations. This book is an excellent example of how Christians can positively engage society to add value for all citizens.

Rev. Antony Oliver, PhD.

President, Caribbean Evangelical Theological Association
Former Principal, Jamaica Bible College, Mandeville, Jamaica
Former Vice President Academic Affairs, CGST, Kingston Jamaica
Former Dean of Academic Affairs, Caribbean Nazarene College, Trinidad

AUTHOR'S PREFACE

I consider this publication an expression of my sacred right to write my opinion on issues relating to life in Trinidad and Tobago. It is also an important aspect of my experience as a minister of religion.

The publication is a chronologically compiled collection of letters to the editor, sent to the opinion page of the local Newsday newspaper, with a few being published by the Trinidad Guardian.

The letters cover a wide range of topics over a period of 25 years. It addresses the obvious lack of commentary by members of the Christian community in the wider media. The traditional model of the church is to speak at the pulpit, but say little, if anything at all, to the community at large.

Generally, expressions have been left to individuals and other groups with differing ideologies. 'Letters to the Editor' in the opinion section have been seen as a place for politicians and academics to argue the issue of the day. This book chronicles some of the letters shared to the newspaper from a Christian perspective.

This author is not preoccupied with the theological, as much as the pragmatic, in presenting ideas and solutions that the church and the community can consider and implement where possible.

The Christian worldview is espoused and interwoven in the letters, as the author seeks to engage readers in considering the Biblical perspective on matters in the public view.

It is hoped that this book will inspire other Christian writers to boldly comment on issues that affect our nation, the region, and the world.

The style of writing is largely 'editorial', covering topics and issues that demanded a response from the Christian segment of society. It is generally expressive, but not necessarily confrontational. The letter speaks to topics that engage readers to rethink their positions on important matters that confront us every day.

Overall, it is a bold attempt to address and shape the opinion of the nation on issues. On a few occasions, there were direct responses to the letters written, including the call for the establishment of an organization to address children's concerns, in the letter titled "Don't suffer little Children" printed on 11/12/2000. The letter was also referred to in a remark by then-President Dr Arthur Robinson, or the call for a "Time to have a place for the steelpan" (7/10/2015), which eventually saw the construction of a facility for the national instrument.

While no full credit can be claimed for these results, the opinions expressed served to add to the concurrent voices of those calling for change and improvement, in one matter or another.

The book 'Letters to the Editor' will be included in the listing of publications in Christian Historical Society, an organization founded by the author.

ACKNOWLEDGEMENTS

To the Editor and team at the NEWSDAY Trinidad and the Trinidad Guardian for kindly publishing my letters, submitted to the editor, throughout these many years.

To my family Marc Anthony, Nadiege Teri-Ann, Solange Chantal, and Dr Shanice Patrice for their timely feedback and responses, to my insistence that they read my letters to the editor on their way to adulthood.

To my many friends and prayer partners in ministry who have been my support throughout this process.

To my dear friend in the ministry, Dr Mark Daniel, for his kind persuasion and encouragement for me to publish a book or two. Smile

To Mr Ronan Ramoutar, a professional photographer for the cover photo.

Above all, my dear Holy Spirit for his leading and guidance in expressing my views.

INTRODUCTION

I have always been someone who speaks out and shares what is on my mind on matters. As a student, I would sit and think through an issue and proffer ideas to the discussion, sometimes in contradiction to the pervading points of view. It was not difficult for me to transition to the mass media of expressing my ideas on the world around me through the medium of the newspaper.

My thoughts expressed are drawn from my responses to situations and occurrences in my environment that impacted my life and those around me.

To be able to share is a cherished opportunity that is hinged on my freedom of speech. I hold this as sacrosanct in the face of God. My book 'Letters to the Editor' reveals my expression of this right over the years.

This compilation includes letters written over 25 years to the newspaper, mainly the Trinidad Newsday, with a few published in the Trinidad Guardian.

My training in journalism and experience in writing for the "Texaco Star", a leading multinational publication of Texaco Trinidad Inc, and other writings, have brought me to the forum; to share my thoughts on various issues.

My Christian worldview was central to all I shared, but my letters also emphasized the importance of the Christian man or woman to actively participate in matters that affect them in the world.

But my most important motivation came from my relationship with my heavenly father. I see these letters as an expression of His grace, and an opportunity to speak 'truth' to the world from a Biblical perspective.

You will find that my style is more journalistic, universal, and not preachy or theological. The message must be shared, and lives impacted by referring to relationships with God, whether subtle or direct. This is not pulpit preaching but a different form of public speaking. Like the Apostle Paul on Mars Hill, it's in the 'marketplace' of our time.

I have sought to address the nation, the national leaders, the community leaders, and the church. The letters became a way for me to speak to the corporate church, on its role and position on important matters.

Not all letters written were sent to the editor for publishing. I have several letters that remained in my files. Sometimes this occurred because of the nature or recency of the issue being addressed. But ultimately, the leading of the Holy Spirit determined what was to be included in this publication.

The letters are placed in chronological order, as they reflect a period of time. They reflect on topics and issues that have been addressed and were current or of a topical theme.

I will continue to share as the Holy Spirit leads, as we all should.

"But in your heart set Christ as Lord being ready always to give a logical defence to anyone who asks you to account for the hope and confident assurance that is within you with gentleness and respect." 1 Peter 3:15 ASV.

MINSHALL HAS CROSSED THE LINE

THE TRINIDAD GUARDIAN
Tuesday, 6th December 1994

Did the articulate and creative bandleader really consider the significance of the term Hallelujah before announcing it as his banner for revelry? The word is definitely a mal appropriation of a wonderful and spiritual term in the lexicon of those of us who share a reverential relationship with God.

All God-fearing people should join in a holy chorus against this desecration of a sacred word that enunciates the potency of our divine God.

It's time to stand against the encroachments of the Lords of hell. The continued hellish preoccupation with revelry has historical precedence in the Biblical chronicles. Need we expand on?

The results of gay abandonment; but more pertinently we must express our abhorrence of the use of the word Hallelujah for embellishing the hellish revelry we know as carnival. (The word Carnival needs little help anyway).

The use of the term Hallelujah is at least irrelevant, and an outright defiance of God and the sacred relationship we should embrace.

Theologically, the word means Praise to Jah; further, it will be a rallying cry for the great multitude in heaven. (Rev 19:1-6) The lord omnipotent reigneth. All who believe, live in anticipation of that great day when the multitude in heaven will sing hallelujah!

For Mr Minshall's information, we are now practising for that great event and encouraging all who listen to join in the holy chorus on earth. The naming of a carnival band as 'Hallelujah' is counter to our purpose. We do not now need an unholy misappropriation of the term in revelry, in what is a direct contradiction of sacred pursuits.

One can argue that a fine line exists between creativity and rationality. There must be some licence to the unbridled use of expressions and appellations such as hallelujah for a Carnival band or any other unrelated activity or pastime.

Let us have some sanity amidst this folly. Let us publicly proclaim our disgust with this flagrant desecration of a pure word.

I belong to a different band, Mr Minshall. Excuse me, but I can't join you in your proclamation here on earth and certainly (if you persist) in the life hereafter. I sing hallelujah here to God only and plan to sing it again up there. Care to join me?

There is also something here to be said about 'the blind leading the blind' The banner hallelujah reflects light in praise to Jah, Jehovah God. Mr Minshall has crossed the line! I hope he and his followers see the light.

The watchmen. (I have set the watchmen on the walls. Isa 62:6)

NEWS

CALL FOR CHRISTIANS TO DECLARE WAR ON CRIME

NEWSDAY

Tuesday, 9th March 1999

A call has gone out for Christians to declare war on crime in Trinidad and Tobago. Rev. Terrence Honoré, leader of the little-known Palmiste Family Fellowship, has made the call in what he said was a response to both the Attorney General and the Prime Minister, who have said that there is a place and function for the church in addressing the ills of society, particularly against the rising incidence of crime.

Speaking to Newsday, he said "Traditionally the church has acted as an important agent in suppression of criminal tendencies by providing a prove deterrent, the Word of God... the Bible. This has been our main weapon, our sword.

"I address the Christian fraternity when I call for a more unified and visual campaign against crime. Christians against Crime can be a rallying cry across the country and all ministers of the gospel should join and intensify our spiritual warfare against crime."

Honoré said he was making no mention, nor seeking to respond to the declarations made by other religious bodies in our society. "That is not our fight, that is a flesh and blood issue. Christians wrestle against spiritual wickedness in high places. That's why our first call of order is to take the 'high' ground. Christians everywhere should meet on the highest point in their country and claim that village, town, or city for Jesus Christ. That's how the battle is won"

Rev. Honoré acknowledged the efforts of the state and the protective service in dealing with crime and said Christians are praying for them thereby using one of their best weapons.

The reverend added, "The evidence of satanic manipulations is manifested in the gruesome nature of recent crimes. We must do more than from a remedial position… rescue the perishing and adopt a more aggressive spiritual strategy.

"It is time to begin a campaign to address this scourge of the society. Prayer and action can and will affect a change. We should chase away the demons that are affecting our communities, our families our wives and daughters...that is our fight"

Rev. Honoré asked that the AG convene a meeting with the Christian community to discuss how they can better assist in launching a new offensive against the stubborn crime problem.

Note: News article written on comments made by the author

DON'T SUFFER LITTLE CHILDREN

NEWSDAY

Monday, December 11, 2000

THE EDITOR:

Christians hold dearly to the words of Jesus Christ, found in Matthew 19:14, where he is recorded as saying, "Suffer the little children to come unto me for such is the kingdom of heaven" With the recent and increasing incidents of violence against children. I fear that some individuals have misinterpreted and misapplied the imperative 'suffer the little children'. Allow me to clear this malapropism, or at least this perception, which may have given rise to this predicament of paediatric violence.

As an English idiom, 'suffer' means simply to allow, to permit. This clearly indicates that we should allow children to be children and to enjoy their childhood, not to be preyed upon by the warped imaginations and evil manipulations of men. Certainly, it does not mean that we should 'cage' their innocence through the mass media or by any other means. It certainly does not mean we should bring suffering to our children's lives.

I call on all sections of this society, particularly the church, to embark on a campaign to shield, protect and nurture our children to counter the violence being meted out to them. And to my brothers, this must go beyond the Sunday School hour. There must be an overt effort to address this problem in our society.

Today's children, deprived of love and attention, will become the angry young men and women of the future, preoccupied with self-destruction and driven by spirits from the darker side. Indeed, if the fabric of the society is the family, then the children are the golden threads that when interwoven with love, serve to create a tapestry of strength and beauty.

The situation, as it is, looks ugly for our children. Someone has tainted the landscape. Each day the newspaper announces another stroke of violence. These accounts are but a brief insight into the horrific problem that confronts us. The stories we read reflect our time, our society, sick and getting sicker.

The prognosis for our children's well-being seems grim, but this prevents the false security of thinking that these are isolated incidents.

Our children are under attack by the many forces that wrestle with diligent mothers and fathers, at their wit's end, to win the war for their minds and hearts. I dare say someone is stealing our children from under our noses. The question is, what are we doing about it?

Certainly, we need to be more protective, more particular, and as parents, to take the necessary time-out to deal with the anger issues in our families and our communities. This then is a call for increased prayer and vigilance on such matters in our society that influence the negative emotions and violence, which seems to be intensifying each day.

Our political rhetoric our first response to situations and issues should be tempered with wisdom, love, and patience. These, when unchecked, give birth to a predisposition for the sort of violence for which we must take collective responsibility. There should be a watchdog organization established with the sole intent of protecting our children from the invasive negative elements of the North American culture and the internet, among other things.

It seems that we have lost the happy times, the good old days. We seem to be losing the battles for the souls of our children. Where are the fun centres, maybe the next government would provide a permanent place for our children to be children, even for a day? Providing a safe, supervised environment to stir up the imagination, maybe our own 'Disney' would do.

There should be more programmes on television, more positive stories, and educational cartoons. We need more preventive measures than remedial events. Our schools and churches must be credited for their valiant efforts to deal with the problem, but we need a more concerted effort for this situation. Let's check the value system and teach good manners again. And for God's sake and our children's, let's address the problem and in the old English let's 'suffer it to be so!!!'

CRIME IS A SPIRITUAL THING

NEWSDAY

Monday, 8th February 2001

THE EDITOR:

Persons who commit crime often confess that they "didn't know what came over them", or they perform the acts in fits of uncontrollable rage. That is one for the psychologists and psychiatrists, but there is another perspective on the crisis of crime that we must consider, and it is simply that crime is a spiritual thing. The Bible declares this.

From the first murder in Genesis to the evidence of organized crime syndicates of our generation to the increasing incidents of crimes among every class of society.

What we have are men who function with a lack of conscience, ensnared by forces from the darker side.

There is no sense of values. No recognition of a divine creator who is personally interested in the affairs of man.

This sense of "lostness" has continued to plague our society as evidenced by the recent spate of horrific crimes that defy any sense of reasoning, as men express their frustrations on each other and increasingly so against women and children.

This is a malady of hopelessness, which yields little ground to the conscientious efforts of our government and other concerned parties.

Our generation has witnessed crimes of all degrees, entire families killed, husband and wives and even children killing children. It is more than the so-called crime of necessity, stealing to survive, to stay alive. As unacceptable as that may be, it pales in comparison to the accounts of the gruesome murders that can only be attributed to the spiritual dimension.

These are the days when the Bible declares that the hearts of men will be failing them for fear. It is evident that the shifting ideologies and decaying morality have given birth to genii (demons) of crime and the reign of the unbridled violence in our land. This may sound extreme, but so indeed is the situation.

What must be done, is for us to first acknowledge that there are those in the spiritual realm that instigate the crimes we witness today.

Some may contend that there are other explanations, such as childhood deprivation, societal pressures, and such like, but this logic is flawed in the context of the escalating incidences of crime.

The question of what we are doing wrong should be replaced by what we should be doing right to address the problem. It is clear that we are not making as much progress as we ought to.

What we need in Trinidad and Tobago is a revival of values based on the Word of God. It's time for the transformation to begin. The crux of the matter is the cross of Jesus Christ. I make no apologies for advocating a dogmatic approach to addressing crime among us. It is the heart of man that change must come. There must be a radical departure from the flagrant disregard for truth, to attitudes that foster love and respect in the family, and consequently, in the nation.

There have been many voices in the society crying for a cessation of crime, a mediation of conflict, resolution of issues, all noble but limited.

For years, the labour movement sang their marching song "We shall overcome" in dealing with exploitation and white-collar crime, that fervour is needed in a united effort to sound a battle cry against crime.

But even that would be inadequate without the required transformation in the collective consciousness of our nation, that indeed, we need God. For while we may psychoanalyse the situation, we must realize that we need the creator in our lives. As my friend and late Christian brother Ras Shorty I sang "we push the creator out', and I declare that we are paying for it.

I am renewing the call I made over two years ago, that Christians should declare war on crime. I repeat my call for believers to unite in prayer and action against crime.

If indeed, we accept it as a spiritual issue, then we are compelled to comply with the spiritual instruction to contend with the spiritual (satanic) principalities and powers that control the minds, hearts, and actions of men.

The church presents both preventative and curative measures to address the problem, but the situation has escalated, and Christians need to intensify their spiritual warfare in a united campaign against crime.

We commend the ongoing efforts of churches and other groups that visit our institutions, counsel families, and assist those who re-join society, but there is much more that can be done.

But there is need for an increased visible contribution by Christians across the land, in support of the new initiative by our police service, in their efforts to deal with crime.

However, what we really need is a wake up for Christians to fight crime. I trust that our government will avail itself of the powerful contributions that prayer and action from Bible-believing Christians can make, in arresting this problem of crime in our nation.

COMMENTARY

LET THE CHURCH ARISE!

NEWSDAY

Monday, 19th April 2001

THE EDITOR:

OUR FIRST Prime Minister, Dr Eric Williams once spoke on the topic 'Role of the Church in our Changing Society', and although I do not recall the date and place, the topic had aroused my interest as a child, and it is still relevant today. I am convinced that we need to revisit the issue of the church and its role in the context of the challenges we face in our society today.

I contend that there is a distinct and definitive role for the church the Body of Christ in dealing with the challenges of our progressive society.

We appreciate from the exegesis of scripture, that the church in its essence and existence is a vibrant dynamic entity, with specific God-given responsibility to effect change and improvement in our country.

Clearly Defined

I write here specifically of those who believe in Jesus Christ, who are brothers regardless of the denominational labels they wear. The role is clearly defined and systematically outlined in the Bible, to provide preventative and remedial measures for improving both our temporal and eternal existence.

At the risk of being presumptuous, I declare that the true conviction of a believer is that the Bible, the Word of God, speaks volumes to us on matters of government, conduct and rectitude in the society.

The Old Testament is replete with examples of governments, authorities, powers, and such matters that provide a wealth of counsel for the prudent inquirer.

We may ask King Solomon of his wisdom and folly. David of his impropriety and triumphs. But pertinently, we could and should learn from the lessons of intrigue and mayhem that the Bible records for our guidance.

In many ways the same 'bacchanal' exists in our society today. There is, after all, nothing new under the sun. Essentially, the issue is how to keep God at the heart of our endeavours, to promote and foster Christian values in our children and our families and to maintain and encourage integrity (truth) in our dealings.

It is the unequivocal role of the church to positively influence and impact on the affairs of our society and the world, to provide the guidelines and counsel to ensure alignment with God's divine plan.at the individual and corporate level.

When we speak of the church, we address not the monolithic, bureaucratic, and manipulative organizations as some are inclined to be, but the dynamic spirit-led institutions of faith in God characterized by demonstrated love and concern for others.

This church has evidenced numerous transformations of lives and families, it is time that we document and research the results of these dramatic changes that are commonplace in the church.

In fulfilling its role, the church must desist from its preoccupation with humanistic, materialistic matriculations, when evaluating the efficacy of its ministry to the community.

It never is a matter of 'numeric' in the Kingdom of God, rather the quality of commitment in Jesus Christ.

The church cannot measure its success by larger buildings and mass media campaigns, but by groups of men and women whose ministries are relevant and effective in dealing with problems in our society.

What apparently obtains now is a secular criterion for success, which seems to be replacing spiritual values as the measure of the man and the ministry. This is wrong. Christians in Trinidad and Tobago need to redefine and refine their position.

In many aspects the church does fulfil its roles, through the sustained prayers of the believers being raised for our land, for those in authority, for governance, for providence.

It is the prayer of the devoted grandmother that has restrained the forces of evil from running rampant through our land.

Our mothers have been praying while our men have been retreating to the rum shops, bars, and television sets.

Our women are tired from having to work to keep bread on the table, or to provide for a home without a father. This is a recipe for disaster, and we are reaping the consequences. That is the crux of the matter. If not prayers, we will have tears.

Lack of prayer

Meanwhile, the escalating crime, the wantonness, the disrespect for authority, all evidence of a rebellious society, attitudes birthed in the fertile soil of discontent and spiritual role abandonment by our men. This pattern must be reversed if we are to ensure a healthy and prosperous nation. The church cannot be part of the problem; it presents the solution.

Indeed, the role of the church in our society is shaped through the family unit, with the parents at the door to ward off. But prayer is not just the responsibility of the man or the praying mother but the entire family. We hear the adage that 'the family that prays together, stays together.' Indeed, the family has become unglued in our society because of the lack of prayer; a lack of devotion to God, and a lack of meaningful spiritual activities.

We must see more of the efforts of the church directed to assisting the community and the nation to effectively deal with our problems. There's need for the church to be more relevant and visible in its ministry to the needs and concerns of the society. This must be consistent with the divine mandate, with programmes and projects designed to assist the fatherless and the widows, the less fortunate as well as those with fortunes.

Nursery For Community

The strategy, therefore, is to identify socio-economic problems and confront then from a Biblical perspective. This is the time for the church's worldview to be enunciated, in politics, economics, sociology, to replace the old models which have failed. It is time for the church to act. To demonstrate the principles taught by Jesus, to impact positively on our society, in fulfilling its mission.

The church is the spiritual citadel of our society, destined to be set upon a hill, to be visible in its activities and forthright in its pronouncements. There is a role for the church in our changing society. The church must change. Not in its essential ecclesiastical nature but in its relevance and influence. The church is indeed a nursery for the community, an institution for the nation, with a divine imperative, to provide light to the darkening minds and souls of men.

Let's see more Christian schools, more programmes for the neglected children, the rejected youths, and dejected adults. The church has solutions for the nation's problems. Dr Eric Williams was right, there is a role for the church in our changing society.

That is, if Christians choose to be what they ought to be, a uniting force of love for our country. Let the Church arise!

Rev. Terrence Honoré is an Executive Member of the Council of Evangelical Churches in Trinidad and Tobago)

COMMENTARY

DELIVER US FROM FREEPORT EVIL

NEWSDAY
Wednesday, 28th March 2001

THE EDITOR:

Something is wrong at Freeport. Not the village that is, but the section of the Solomon Hochoy highway which passes through the area. There have been at least 60 vehicular deaths along a 200-metre stretch on either side of the flyover. We cannot continue to 'drive by' the chilling statistics of 15 deaths in a year, and three to five accidents each month!

The number of accidents is told and retold by the villagers, of vehicles racing off, slamming into each other, and changing lanes and even plunging between the rails to the road beneath. Stories like the driver who suddenly lost control of his vehicle, which somersaulted several times before landing on its wheels and speeding off. Or another who drove along the embankment parallel to the south-bound lane, clearing railings as he went, and crossing the main road, before fatally crashing into a lamp post on the other embankment.

It is said that the highest number of recorded deaths on the highway has been recorded at the Freeport fly-over. It may well be a death trap for commuters on their way home. The traffic authorities indicated that there have been over 100 mishaps registered in the area, not to mention the numerous collisions and near-fatal mishaps. If we were to place crosses at the sites where people died, there would be little room for one to pass!

Several years ago, while driving home one night from a university class, I saw a Mazda RX7, a small fast car of the 1980s, suddenly veer right, out of control, striking the guard rails and overturning. I pulled over and rushed to the scene to see a young man climb out, he was obviously injured, while a woman in her late fifties sat nearby groaning in pain from a fractured femur. The car had come to a stop on top of the fly-over bridge and soon enough the village rescue team, an unofficial group I'm sure, was on the scene. No doubt they would have assisted many persons over the years.

Historically, the area holds no secrets. It was once part of an old coffee estate. A small pond was located at the base of what is now the northbound lane. Nothing could be deduced from these simple facts to provide an explanation for the incidents. However, current records are full of documented details, which give one an uneasy feeling that something is just not right in this situation.

Recently, my family and I were heading south and had topped the fly-over when we heard a loud noise from the underside of the car. I slowed and applied the brake at the same time, trying to identify the sound. When we pulled aside some distance away, I discovered that my left mudguard had become stuck on the tyre and caused the sound that had really startled us. I wondered then, and still do now, how could a relatively firm mud guard fold upwards into the tyre and get stuck there? After all, we had not encountered any rough surfaces along the twenty kilometres of the highway we had previously passed. Strange indeed.

Stranger yet, the stories told by the villagers. The tale of a driver who lost control of his vehicle on the southbound lane and 'flew' over the northbound lane before landing on the street below, some 20 feet away. He was killed instantly. Or the man who is convinced that he saw someone standing in front of his vehicle as he approached the fly-over. He swung away to avoid him. His car was wrecked. This particular report, I am told, was mentioned by several individuals who were involved in accidents in the area.

Even more intriguing, is the tale of a man who pulled over to park on the shoulder of the northbound lane a few metres from the flyover, intent on investigating an accident on the southbound lane. In his attempt to cross over and check out the carnage on the other side, he was struck and killed by an oncoming vehicle. Two deaths within minutes.

What has caused these deaths? Is it an increase in the number of vehicles, excessive speeding, or a combination of both? These are plausible explanations, but not conclusive since not all cases fit this profile. In the late '70s and '80s, there were two distinct incidents related by personal friends. On both occasions, they were well within the speed limit and just a few metres from the fly-over, when a car from the opposite lane suddenly rushed across the median and struck them. In both instances the vehicles were 'totalled', and occupants suffered injuries. They were both safe drivers.

This submission is not to recount the 'gross' details of death on the Freeport fly-over, but to raise an inquiry of some sort, at least a question or two, as to why people are dying at this particular section of the highway. One wonders if the authorities have looked beyond the obvious to identify other causes. Is it technical, metaphysical, or spiritual? An engineer friend once explained that the road leading to the fly-over is banked at an angle, which causes speeding vehicles to veer off to the right, due to an increase in the centripetal force. Vehicles come into contact with the railing that separates the lanes, and many have plunged down to the road beneath. Is it possible that there exists a technical fault in the construction of the Freeport fly-over? This should be investigated.

There might be some merit to the 'engineering' theory, as a similar situation exists at the Gasparillo fly-over several miles to the south, which runs second in the number of deaths recorded in the history of the highway. At least 25 fatal accidents and numerous incidents have been recorded.

These are the only two areas along the highway, where the statistics of vehicular deaths have steadily risen over the years. Some sort of warning signs should be installed in this area. Maybe a 'reduce speed zone' should be introduced or special markings placed on the highway.

Recently, I came upon a road-paving crew. They were busy repairing the road leading up to the Freeport fly-over. The new surface looked good, but I was certain it could not cover the blood of the many that died along that fateful stretch of highway. My condolences to all who lost loved ones at the location.

One villager lamented,' There's too much blood in the area. Too many people died. He referred to the death of two persons just a few days before. It seems, he said, that people are dying there every month. He could shed no light on the causes of the alarming statistics, although he had lived in the area for over 65 years.

Is it that the Freeport fly-over is a port to the 'other side'? How else can we explain the startling statistics of deaths and the numerous accidents that have occurred in the area? One of the early deaths on the highway was a young man who went to test drive his modified sports car… he never returned home alive.

There must be evil there, I conclude. As a God-fearing man, I believe that evil exists and someone or something has contributed to the notorious nature of that section of the highway. There are spiritual forces that have taken residence in the area. I call on my Christian brothers to join me in prayer at Freeport and Gasparillo, as I am convinced that there is a need for some spiritual deliverance.

Maybe someone would otherwise proffer an explanation on how to reverse the trend or stop the fatalities that occur in the area. As for me, whenever I approach the Freeport fly-over in particular, I say a prayer and drive with care.

TIME FOR A CHRISTIAN MANIFESTO

NEWSDAY

Tuesday, 2nd January 2001

THE EDITOR:

For many, Christianity and politics don't mix. The concepts have been on the opposite sides of the fence in traditional Pentecostal thinking. But the recent statements by Pastors Cuffie and Bachew demonstrate a growing intent among Christians to express their clear position on political matters. I am certain, though, that some individuals may take offence to the remarks made by both pastors in support of their political party of choice for the now concluded general elections.

But my real interest here is not to debate with Rev Cuffie or Pastor Bachew, but to indeed raise another related issue. It may not have been enunciated by my brothers, but there is a distinct and definitive position and role for Christians on matters of government and the functions of the state. It is the fundamental view of born-again Christians, that we possess a divine mandate as presented in the Bible. I submit, that not only is there a mandate to promote and propagate the Word of God but to represent His divine position on issues of civil society. The church the Body of Christ has a clear mandate.

Although this may come as a surprise to some of us, the Bible is clear in its guidance on every possible issue under the sun. The Bible is complete. It is replete with examples of good and bad governments of ancient civilizations. May I suggest that what the Bible presents is more a God-festo rather than a mani-festo? And certainly, the Christian manifesto, the Bible, outlines and emphasizes all that pertains to Godliness and righteous living. The issues which confront us in our communities have relevant and ready solutions in the Bible. The call for integrity in office, honesty in business, and equity in dealing with different ethnic groups in a pluralistic society are all amplified in the Bible. Christ's handling of the racially charged situation with the Samaritan woman attests to this fact, which he spoke with her in contravention of the popular prejudice of the day.

I dare say that all political parties and interest groups can glean much from the Bible on issues of national importance, particularly matters of forgiveness and reconciliation. I endorse the call made by the Prime Minister for greater involvement by Christian (Pentecostals) in politics. We must move from a state of passivity to divinely inspired activity. Albeit there are many Christians who are key members of the political parties to indeed, 'render to Caesar' (the state) the things that are 'Caesar's' the bread and fish issues can be successfully addressed.

The Christian manifesto presents guidelines for all earthly plans and introduces measures for long-term strategic planning that are literally out of this world. The eternal is essential in considering our actions, plans, and deliberations. Our very words will condemn us, if not uttered in consultation with God and in the context of love and mutual respect.

Yes, Mr. Prime Minister, Christians have a manifesto too. We are admonished to pray for those in authority, for the peace of the land for righteousness in government, and we have adhered to that instruction. The other side of this is speaking out on issues when they come into conflict with the Word of God. In this regard, we have been reticent. The church has been too silent on issues and should express the basic tenets of scripture whenever possible. It is our 'manifest destiny' to proclaim the soundness of Biblical values to our nation.

Certainly, the nation will be hearing more from Pentecostal Christians. Not just the few who seem to speak for the rest, but the growing numbers of young people intent on fulfilling their God-given mandate to contribute to the development of our nation-state.

I can assure the Prime Minister that Christians have been meeting. Position papers are forthcoming on economics, education, and other related issues from organizations like the Trinidad and Tobago Council of Evangelical Churches, among others.

And so, every Christian in every community and indeed in every political party must first follow their divine mandate in the order of things. I dare say that various elements things of the manifesto, and the Bible can be applied to provide the foundation for the national transformation of man and the nation.

Christians are not only in the churches, but they are in the political parties. Our prayers, commitment, and overall involvement are demonstrative of our conscientious interest in the development of our nation.

Our contributions to the community have been the underpinning for many successful endeavours. Yet, there is room for more overt presence and action by Christians in upholding the Word of God and its interpretation for resolving issues in our country. The Christians in our midst, those who pray, who work with the downtrodden and depressed. The many unsung heroes who counsel guide and encourage families, helping to keep the fabric of our society together. We will continue to do what we must. Our ministries and many small churches will continue to make contributions to our society. To put it plainly, party in party out, the church has a higher calling.

I admonish all Christians to be prompt in declaring the word of God, in speaking out on issues and being directly involved in all honesty and positive attempts to guide the direction our country is taking on our road to progress. With 'manifesto' in hand, we stand in prayer and action for our land.

COMMENTARY

PALMISTE... PRESERVE THE HISTORY

NEWSDAY

Tuesday, 6th February 2001

THE EDITOR:

For over ten years there has been a quiet but concerted effort to appeal to the authorities to consider the establishment of a historical museum site at Palmiste, in San Fernando. The area represents the only remaining site of a sugar factory in the south (other than that of Ste Madeleine of course).

In the map of 1889, prepared by Antilles Petroleum Company Limited, the Palmiste estate consisted of several smaller estates including Cedar Grove, Phillipine, Canaan, Bel Air, La Resource, and Bachelors Hall. The area still bears the name of some of these sites while others have been lost in the transition.

However, despite the many changes over the years, some relics of the past are still identifiable at various points throughout the community.

Today, one can still see the remnants of a small bridge, which served the trains transporting sugarcane to feed the nearby factory.

It is not uncommon for homeowners in the Palmiste area to find the large ten-foot cistern in their back yards, part of the water collection system of the past. They remain there, too costly to relocate, too precious to destroy.

Miles of rails were cut and used as fence posts for the nearby Palmiste Park. Elsewhere in the area, the chimney of the once proud factory stands, now overgrown with weeds and clingers, but a proud sentinel of the past.

The ongoing quest is to persuade the relevant authorities to support the identification and release of the Palmiste factory as a site worthy of restoration, preservation, and exhibition. The problem has been compounded by the difficulties in securing approvals by the custodians of the property.

Altogether, I have continued to be seriously disappointed in the way we treat our history. As a people, we need to pick up the pride of our heritage, in this case, the celebration of the era when sugar was king and held out its sweet sceptre to our fledging society.

We cannot continue to overlook the significance of emphasizing the importance of our past for the benefit of our children and the future. We have to stop trampling the remnants of our heritage under the guise of progress and indiscriminately destroying or disregarding the voices of our past which speaks volumes to us if we could only listen.

The Palmiste Historical Society is being formed to champion this cause. We join other few but encouraging efforts like the Caribbean Historical Society and the recently formed Petrotrin Historical Society. Our mission is to restore, preserve, and exhibit the historical sites at Palmiste.

Indeed, we must appreciate what went before, learn from it, and share the knowledge with children. Our students can visit and visualize the past and gain vital insights into that popular period of our history. They will then be less inclined toward that popular period of our history. They will then be less inclined to appreciate somebody else's history more than their own as they are so readily inclined to do.

With the recent interest in museums and historical sites, one hopes that this appeal would gain sanction and support from the powers that be. The Palmiste Historical Society will certainly be a complement to the beauty of the recently Palmiste National Park, with its heart-shaped pond and landscaped slopes.

This is a call to preserve Palmiste and all other communities. It is a call for us to have a greater sense of pride in our places of interest, not only for ourselves but also for our children and our children's children.

WISDOM FOR OUR PROBLEMS

NEWSDAY

Tuesday, January 2, 2001

THE EDITOR:

In celebration of our 50th year of independence, we must take time to consider the many problems that plague our nation, but while we celebrate, we must get to the root cause of our problems.

I recently read an interesting quotation that would help us to shed some light on our many challenges.

It came from a man who has been admired by many and makes for good reading even today.

"The roots of our problems are wealth without work, pleasure without conscience, knowledge without character, commerce without morality, science without humanity, worship without sacrifice, politics without principles." – Mohandas K Gandhi

How applicable, how relevant. Let's apply and pray.

ENDEMIC PROBLEM OF EPIDEMIC PROPORTIONS

NEWSDAY

Tuesday, January 8, 2014

THE EDITOR:

There must be some kind of international index to gauge the security of life in Trinidad and Tobago, with the rampant, wanton crimes that have plagued our country in recent years.

Even so, there should be some kind of parallel to consider what strategies are adopted by PAHO and the world organisations in situations of epidemics. Our country is in an unhealthy state.

What we have been facing is no isolated domestically instigated, gang-originated or returning-deportee manifestation of crime in our country. This is an endemic problem of epidemic proportions that does not seem to go away. A cancer that seems to have no cure, a malady with no apparent remedy.

How the landscape of our country has changed from train and cane to bush and stumps, from the picturesque pastoral scenes of the past to a country choked by thorns and thistles of violence. The Bible speaks of a country that "suffers violence daily". This, Trinidad and Tobago, is what we have become.

Yet, like the fabled phantom cartoon, many have ridden on a horse called "hero" trying to catch the criminals and rid the country of crime. Others have resorted to being great fishermen purporting to catch the "big fish" criminals, but to no avail. And we still have places in our jails, albeit in a neglected and confused state.

So, I write, because like many citizens in our beloved country I feel the pain. But not everybody it seems feels the pain of the loss... of the carnage of life. Many have become so accustomed to the deaths, so effectively printed in gory detail, that we are not shocked or not for too long, at the severity or frequency of the crimes. Every single crime should awaken the passionate caring human being in each of us so that we should resolve to observe, detect, and report crime and criminal activity.

I am not a military man, but there must be a broad-based campaign to address crime in our country. Each street, village, and town should set up crime watch groups financed by the government and well organised to launch grassroots battles against this "epidemic".

The fight against crime knows many fronts. The true soul of the matter is the hearts and minds of the people of Trinidad and Tobago, especially our children and youth. They are exposed to the violence and abuse. Our children are as much the victims of crime as our adults!

An initiative should be launched to educate children and youths on the scourge of crime. A mandatory seminar should be conducted in each school, each term for at least a year. There should be a special week of deliberations at tertiary institutions, dedicated to "Considerations on the Reduction of Crime in Trinidad and Tobago".

Employers should engage workers in discussions on the negative effects of white-collar crime. Like in industry, there should be a national record of the number of days without a crime.

Churches should have a coordinated collective prayer effort that cuts across the insularity and apparent lack of unity. They have been too silent and have demonstrated little overt efforts at reducing crime. Where is the 40-day national fast like the Israelites of old?

I advocate that emphasis should be placed on the "soft approach". Seek to arrest the decay in the society by addressing the issue in the minds of young people.

Many years ago, there was a national campaign to address the garbage problem with the symbol "Charlie", so why can't we implement a national crime containment strategy to address this problem?

NEWS

WHITHER THE WIDOWS

NEWSDAY

Tuesday, 24th June 2014

THE EDITOR:

I must first commend the relevant authorities, and indeed the Honourable Chief Justice Ivor Archie, for the recent announcement concerning benefits accorded to widows of retired judges. It is a commendable and caring move, biblical in its connotation, as it echoes the important instructions given to the Church to 'consider' the widows in our midst.

But, like many among us, I am also concerned about the welfare of the other 39,749 or more widows listed in our national census of 2011. Many widows, whose concerns and conditions remain marginal and unattended.

It seems, with all the challenges facing our country, the care and attention to widows seemed to have been relegated to the bottom of the "totem pole". Never making it to the top of the list on the political platform, but they remain "constants" that are fundamental to the continuance of civil society. I speak pointedly of the rights and privileges of the many widows in our community.

I was recently moved by the thought that, yet another prominent professional passed on, and there was silently no mention of his wife, except to say she is now a widow. She is not in the picture, even though she had been with him throughout his illustrious career, as an esteemed judge. It would seem as in most cases that when the husband dies, some of the wife's life dies with him.

I am concerned that the position of "widow" brings with it silent suffering. Friends, family, and colleagues would encourage, but things are not the same. Such is life. The extent of this fact is that there are over 245 million widows all over the world, with 211 living in poverty. (United Nations Statistics)

So, we contend with crime. The acts are visible and even gruesome, but the silent suffering of "advantaged" widows remains unheralded and invisible to the masses. Some say suffer it to be so. The reality of the issues affecting widows has received scant consideration.

Who really considers the rights of widows in our country? We need a national status report and relevant action regarding the plight of widows.

We can introduce programs to monitor the status of widows and ensure that grief counselling and financial support are accorded to those who are according to scripture "are widows indeed".

However, Christians are compelled, even mandated in the model of the 1st century Church, not to neglect widows. While there have been many quiet efforts to assist widows in the local community, there have been no "published" efforts for widows in the contemporary church.

The Church should take the lead as an institution of care, to visibly and openly provide support and advocacy for widows. Much success can be achieved in collaboration with the state and civil society agencies, to ensure that widows do not 'slip through the "social net" of our sometimes-callous society.

WITHOUT SOUTH, THERE CAN BE NO NORTH

TRINIDAD GUARDIAN
Wednesday, 8th January 2014

THE EDITOR:

Over the years, I have noted an unrelenting effort, albeit discrete, to relegate the activities and achievements of people from the south of the country to a "lesser status" than people of "northern origin." It is common knowledge that many residents from the north have an extremely difficult time mentally adjusting to "going down South," or at least even going any further than the Caroni bridge. To some, it is a painful proposition!

Yet it remains, that southerners have no such compunction, having to go up north for their very existence. Braving the weather and unbearable traffic to do business in the north, or to access the maze of government offices needed to be visited to transact their affairs. So, the point of this discussion is that there is a fallacy that has been perpetuated, that what goes on north of the country is superior or better or more rewarding than what happens in the south.

Nothing "down south but bush" has been the cry of many of my northern friends. This might have accounted for the many who moved to the north in the post-1970 migration, when certain communities, like Palmiste in the south, were vacated as many moved to communities in the east and northwest of the country.

But it still remains that "South" has continued to make a considerable contribution to the progress of our beautiful country. Without the South, there will be no North. With the input from the energy sector and other industries, the south continues to produce for east, west, south, and north and the other Caribbean islands as well. As the records show, outstanding contributions have been made in every facet of our nation's development. Let's give credit where credit is due.

In sports, for example, we have achievers like Hasely Crawford (first Olympic gold medallist), Rodney Wilkes (first Olympic medallist), Mansingh Amarsingh (Caribbean table tennis champion), Raphick Jumadeen (West Indies cricketer) and the late Manny Ramjohn, to name a few. Even the first Ombudsman came from Princes Town, and the late former Chief Justice Sir Isaac Hyatali (San Fernando) and writer/historian Michael Anthony from Mayaro.

In music, Ras Shorty I, Machel Montano, Kees Dieffenthaller, Faye Lyons, and there was Sundar Popo and so many others including businessmen, educators, artists, and ministers of religion. Then there is Naparima College, with the distinction of being the first secondary school in the country.

Above all, we proudly acknowledge that three presidents and three prime ministers including our first female prime minister have come from the south. If there is still a problem with appreciating the south then let's consider the gifted people who live "south of South" in places like Point Fortin, Moruga, and Cedros. The talents run deep.

So next time you venture to talk about or visit the south, you should proudly say are we "going up south." That might be more appropriate. I am just making a cardinal point.

THE COUNTRY 'AYO', DON'T LET TREASURY GO TOO

NEWSDAY

Tuesday, 15th April 2014

THE EDITOR:

The kite-flying season is here again. I thought it interesting to consider this seasonal event in light of the current winds of change that have been buffeting our country. It seems to me like this country ayo!

The Bing dictionary describes the word ayo as "loose and flying away: describes a kite when the string is cut, and it flies away quickly". I used the word as a child. I never thought of its meaning, but it's applicable today.

As children, we learned to make various kites, singing angels, common kites, and the dreaded mad bull. What a time! What a season are we facing as a nation!

Recently, one local organization announced their 15th year of celebrations in kite flying, keeping the tradition alive. Great, I thought, but who is to keep our country on course for greatness? With all the violence and moral decay... looseness at carnival and otherwise, it seems like the country simply ayo!

We are lacking in civility (took corruption instead from our colonial past) and messing up our morality (borrowed all the bad from our northern neighbours, neo-colonialism). We are now becoming world famous for our lewd public behaviour and pornographic-type portrayals.

What can be said about this situation? As children, we would hold our heads and cry "kite ayo!" That's when our crafty kite that took us hours to make (with our mother's flour and copy book page) suddenly and regrettably gets loose and flies away. We would run for blocks to find it, stuck in a large tree, or hopefully lying on the ground.

But the chase was on. That's what we need to do as a country, commitment to the ideals of civil society and tenacity to chase down what we lost. We lost control of the sacred cords of honesty, integrity, and neighbourly love.

We need to reconnect with God and the values that build our nation and keep it flying high. We have the skills, knowledge, and abilities to do it. Our history as a nation records the contributions of Rienzi, Butler, Sir Ellis Clarke and so many others. So where are those among us with the "pedigree" to help us maintain high standards?

It seems like "White-collar democracy" prevails when people feel that they are free to bribe and pocket money. There is a day of reckoning coming. There is always a price to pay. Let me borrow something else from the Chinese… a proverb "If a string has an end, then it has another end" But I think the Bajans say it better "Time longer than twine." I hear we are having some favourable winds these days, so let's hold on to the purse strings of the economy, we need to keep it tight and not let the treasury "ayo" too!

NEWS

ROUGH WEATHER ON SEA AND LAND FOR TT

NEWSDAY

Friday, 9th January 2015

THE EDITOR:

As a country, it would seem that we are experiencing a rough-weather time on the land. I speak of the relentless wave of crime that seems to be turning into a tsunami.

This is added to the flood of violence that has inundated our small country. What a state we are in.

It looks like we are in for some rough weather, on sea and on land. With the upcoming general election, people are jumping from ship to ship, trying to get a safe and trustworthy vessel to ride out the storms. Others are seeking to be ship-shape for the turbulent times ahead. Things look grim.

Then there's the economics of scale: we can't seem to balance the books, with the finance minister recently trying to find his "sea legs" on a shifting fiscal deck. The ship of state is being tossed to and fro by the dips and troughs of changes in crude oil prices. The receding waves are set to leave us stranded on our supposed secure high ground. Well, it's more wetting we are getting.

The Government is charting yet another course and is soon to announce a "new" way forward. We are living on a "wing and a prayer". Many are trying to ride the waves, hoping for calmer seas in 2015, but things are looking bleak for the new year. It is hopeless, helpless, with leaks in our security system, non-extradition moves, with a big party on deck while the ship is in distress. The carnivores of crime are still eating away at the soul of the nation ... and the music plays on.

So, the weather forecast for TT looks grim for 2015. More dark clouds are on the horizon. The Met Office can only predict or forecast weather, but not control it.

My real concern is, however, where are the "spiritual met officers", the prophets in our midst? Men and women of God who can hear from God and bring a word to the nation?

The silence from the Christian prophets and seers is deafening, drowning out the cries for divine intervention. People are praying for deliverance and getting shot instead. We need to hear from God. The journey of life in TT is characterised by the reducing life expectancy, as the waves of violence bruise our consciences each day. These are perilous times.

Some prophets need to find their spiritual radar and report. They have to stop letting other ministers and church leaders deter them from speaking the word of God in our time. This is a call to the prophetic few, the righteous crew, to say what must be said.

Why whisper pronouncements in a back room while the blood of murder victims cries out for justice?

So, as we continue to pray for a spiritual respite, we have to "batten down the hatches" (as the old sailors used to say). Both economically and spiritually, we have to keep things on an even keel, as we hold fast to the masts of salvation and truth. That's the only way to ride out this storm.

THE CHURCH NEEDS TO DO MORE FOR THE POOR AND ILL

NEWSDAY

Thursday, 12th February 2015

THE EDITOR:

While we are busy caring for the spiritual health of our charges, we seem to be neglecting the many who need our attention in matters relating to physical and emotional health and well-being.

Given that traditionally the church focused on "soul-saving" and ensuring that people are "well enough" to make it to heaven, there needs to be more organised programmes and activities to address health and wellness issues in our communities.

The traditional hymn, "It is well with my Soul" is a testament to the fact that caring for the soul is the primary responsibility of the Christian Faith. However, we should remember that Jesus Christ also demonstrated that we should offer even more when He fed the multitudes as recorded in the Bible. (St John 6 :1-14).

So, while there are many who provide some form of contribution to the "safety net" for the underprivileged and poor, the effort is unheralded, and a collective effort is certainly needed. There is little evidence of churches contributing individually or collectively to the physical health and wellness issues among people in the community.

Those who question this position should well be reminded that we must make "full proof" of our ministries. The period of service in silence must be replaced by reports of the healthy man "walking and leaping and praising God".

One local minister is set to open a home for single unwed mothers. It might well be one of the few such efforts in the country. Historically, this was a priority for the early missionaries of some of the leading organisations.

So concerned was another minister that she went out and started "Highway and Hedges" to distribute food to the poor and underprivileged in villages across the country. The Church definitely has a role to play in caring for the unwell.

Then, there are organisations which encourage volunteers to travel to other countries, to contribute to care efforts among the poor and sick, while we continue to be limited in our organised efforts among evangelical churches here at home.

It is well known that some of the larger traditional organisations are filled with health professionals who could be challenged to minister to the sick in our midst... that is outside the health institutions and private practices. The Church needs to mature in its service outside of its four walls.

This continuing and improved effort by the church should be directed by those whom God has gifted and trained for such a purpose under the leadership of the ministers and elders.

Over the years, one well known organisation has demonstrated the fulfilment of the need for caring, with health seminars, scholarships, and facilities. The evangelical fraternity has to collectively address the issues affecting the overall health and wellbeing of our country. We must minister to our people in spirit, soul, and body!

Although it is theologically sound to say that spiritual health leads to wellness of the mind, soul, and body, we also acknowledge that the poor we will always have with up. This includes those with poor health.

So, a little talk, a little television programme, and a little seminar is inadequate to address the problem. The Church has to accept a greater responsibility of carrying the load, the "burden of disease" that affects our country.

I look forward to being part of the launch of a "Care Campaign" for churches to make a significant impact on the health and wellness of the communities. So let the streetside healings begin, let the shouts of multiple miracles echo across the land...let the Church arise!!

CALL DAY OF PRAYER AND THANKSGIVING, MR PM

NEWSDAY

Wednesday, 16th September 2015

THE EDITOR:

Our new Prime Minister would do well to take his Cabinet to church. As they set the framework for new governance, they must remember there is no foundation that will last unless it is based on prayer and thanksgiving.

(Except the Lord build the house they labour in vain that build it — Ps127:1) I speak to the leadership of this great party as they celebrate the victory in the recent election and set about their tasks, that they should call on the name of Jesus to set things right. He is the unseen and unnamed member of the Cabinet.

He promised never to leave nor forsake if we call on His name.

I know Dr. Keith Rowley is a God-fearing man, therefore I call on him and his team to take this humble advice and call a day of prayer and thanksgiving for the nation.

Get all the people who pray to pray. Get the nation to declare a holy fast so that we will be governed by the Lord of Hosts, the spirit of La Trinite. This country must be a holy land unto God.

Christian leaders should set aside 40 days of prayer and fast for the new administration. This is not the time for small talk and small prayer.

The blood of the innocent is crying out to God from the ground for right judgement. The violence in the streets has risen and God has responded and put Dr. Rowley in office. We must now honour Him for the victory and for "the wisdom to lead aright." How busy we can be with the work at hand, while keeping the hounds at bay? How dreadful the monsters of economic problems and the myriad number of spirits that are in control in our land. They command our high grounds; they steal our children.

We must pray, Mr Prime Minister, we must pray.

The problems we face as a nation cannot be resolved only through the intelligence of man.

Many well-intentioned technocrats have missed the mark, many have entered politics to make a change, but succumbed to the wickedness of our times. But God has a plan. The secrets for the success of State require a divine connection.

As Prime Minister, Rowley spoke of the accountabilities of office, but we need to remember we are all accountable to Almighty God. We must remove the demons of corruption, violence and racism that have found an equal place in our land.

What we need is more than to say a prayer here and there. We must set things in order on the path of righteousness to exalt our nation.

I call on the Prime Minister to set the right tone, to put God in front, and call for a day of prayer and thanksgiving. This should be his first order of business.

And may God bless our nation.

TURN TO PRAYER TO ARREST CRIME

NEWSDAY

Saturday, 31st October 2015

THE EDITOR:

They will have some comfort in the fact that the Government has allocated the largest portion in the 2015-2016 Budget to the Ministry of National Security.

The police now have more money to better finance their crime-fighting efforts.

They can now spend more time in detection and apprehension leading to conviction.

Consequently, we expect the number of arrests to increase.

But the people of TT must realise the police can't do it alone and give support. As in the Garden of Eden, it doesn't matter who picked or ate the apple, but the consequence is that the human race is paying the price for the infraction.

We all share the burden, the consequences of crime. There are no unaffected bystanders here.

I am convinced that most of our law enforcement personnel are conscientious and dedicated, but their performance has been negatively affected by a few "maladies", some not of their own making.

These issues have contributed in part to the low number of arrests in recent years.

One such condition is the "shortened arm of the law" syndrome that affects officers.

Too many perpetrators have escaped because the long arm of the law was unable to grab hold of them.

I expect that the increased allocation of funds will address this shortcoming.

Another issue is an apparent vision problem. This relates to the process of detection and has been a concern for many years.

Even looking at it from a Canadian viewpoint, has not cleared up the problem.

It remains a serious challenge. But I can see a change coming in the number of arrests that will be made.

In the past, the work of the police was blind-sided when the intelligence unit, SAUTT, was disbanded.

It is now history that there was further short-sightedness due to the delaying of the acquisition of vessels (OPVs) to assist in surveillance of the shady coastline of the Gulf of Paria.

It is crystal clear that one can't achieve good conviction if one can't have good detection.

But with improved resources, the number of arrests is sure to increase.

Then there were the psychologically depressing experiences of not being able to catch "big fish" criminals; with so many legal loopholes in the net, even the small fry got away.

The fishing season was out for the last five years. But now we are anticipating a turning of the tide and opportunities for the law enforcers to apprehend some big fish in their dragnet. We expect a good haul to take to the courts.

It's stressful for our cops to stand by and see people looting our coffers, while their hands are tied by "out-of-time" procedures and their vision obscured due to inadequate resources.

We want to admonish the hardworking police officers not to take "a rest" but to do their best to make arrests.

Also, if the police arm is too short, they need to be reminded of the scripture, "Surely the arm of the Lord is not too short to save, nor his ear too dull to hear" (Isaiah 59:1).

And on the vision issue, "The eyes of the Lord are upon the righteous, and his ears are open unto their cries, but the face of the Lord is against those who do evil" (Ps 34:15).

So, we must now lodge an appeal to the highest order. We need divine intervention and the corporate action to complement it.

Mr. Commissioner, we have to pray.

Our policemen should not raise their hands in despair but raise their hands in prayer. Today they need to pray to hear what God is saying to resolve this matter.

It's time for us to turn to the spirituality factor.

Let's establish a prayer programme in the Police Service, with chaplains and prayer sessions. That is long overdue. So, while our police dutifully look into prevention measures and solving all the red, black, or white-collar crimes, they need to remember to look up to God. Let's pray to reduce this scourge of crime on our land. It's time to arrest crime.

TIME TO HAVE PLACE FOR THE STEELPAN

NEWSDAY

Wednesday, 7th October 2015

THE EDITOR:

I want to applaud the story in Monday's *Newsday*, which reported the comments made by the manager of BP Renegades Steel Orchestra, Michael Marcano, who was quoted as saying the steel pan is a "magnificent gift of God". But there are many God-given gifts we abuse, misuse, or lose, and the steelpan is no exception.

There is a close step from its celebrated status to the dustbin; the same drum is otherwise used for waste collection in our country.

It seems the pan has lost its place among the echelons of symbols of nationalism. It has to be used for more than just people throwing waste in at Carnival or any other time.

I have long lamented the poor treatment meted out to the steelpan, the instrument that plays out the tunes of our patriotism. We continue to disrespect the pan, the inventors and all the hardworking people who have fought valiantly over the years to get the pan to the level of respect it deserves.

The absence of an appreciation centre or museum for the instrument really has me "basodee". I had hoped that one day I would wake up from this nightmare and see a true edifice to the pan.

Somewhere in this God-blessed country we have to find a way to re-write the forsaken story of the pan. We have to do better at the way we treat one of the true pillars of our national heritage. We have to stop talking and act.

A renewed effort by the pan aficionados and enthusiasts could sway the powers that be to get a suitable place for the pan. It would seem the national pan organisation can't make a note when it comes to getting the Government to take the pan to the next level.

Many proposals have been made over the years, notable ideas for national representation of the sacred pan, but it seems like these have played out like a repeat on a musical scoresheet. Our national leaders seemed tone deaf to the cries of our champions of the pan.

One would hope this appeal would strike a favourable chord with the new administration.

We have failed in the past to raise a place for the pan, a home where our children can visit and share in the pride of the historic and cultural significance of the creation of this remarkable instrument.

This seems to be a missing element in our repertoire of nation-building efforts. It's time for a crescendo.

As a youth I was excited when a pan soloist was introduced at my home church in Marabella. It was amazing, revolutionary, and promising.

The practice never caught on.

Today, there are but a few established efforts at schools or churches.

There has not been a broadening of the appreciation for the national instrument and its use in worship.

Every church should have a tenor pan in its worship. The early missionaries brought their accordions and Hawaiian guitars and tambourines, but we have not seen a corresponding use of the cuatro or the steel pan in places of worship. By God's grace we need to make a stand and promote the use of the pan. It should be on the school curriculum and all places of worship.

I call on the Minister of Tourism do something nice, let it be a surprise.

Let our people stand proudly in this blessed land and raise their hands in celebration to the music of the steelpan. Let's have a place for the pan.

NEWS

ROUNDABOUT NATION THAT'S T&T

NEWSDAY

Saturday, 21st November 2015

THE EDITOR:

But we need to apply this consideration, not only to our persistent problems but to the proliferation of roundabouts on the roads.

There are many myths and facts about roundabouts, including that they cause longer commutes, they are difficult to manoeuvre, and are not good for pedestrians and cyclists.

But it seems the good outmanoeuvres the bad.

In the US, for example, over 600 new roundabouts have been built since 1990, according to the Seattle Times.

Some modern roundabouts have been regulated by traffic lights, stop-and-yield signs or even police officers on duty. Many countries have adopted roundabout solutions to their traffic problems.

France, for instance, has over 15,000 roundabouts.

While I am not qualified to evaluate the efficacy of the roundabout, I can certainly comment on the peak traffic "commesse" that occurs at some of our roundabouts.

Letters to the Editor

But there is something to be said about the large number of roundabouts on the nation's roadways. It would seem the roundabout is a fad that we can't get fed-up with, or a quick fix to a traffic situation.

As a child, I enjoyed the way a roundabout worked, with people stopping respectfully to permit others to pass or long lines moving along with ease.

One would think it's practical and progressive to install overpasses or "clover leafs" to ensure a continuous flow and reduce the loss of productive time in long unnecessary traffic lines.

Admittedly, in some areas like St James and other inner-city areas it is indispensable.

The Mon Repos roundabout in San Fernando would enjoy having the Naparima- Mayaro Road pass overhead instead of the consistent stress from letting others "push and pass".

The Pointe-a-Pierre roundabout is so much in the way that numerous cars have driven straight across it on dark nights.

Recently, I was bemused by the construction of a roundabout along the Claude Noel Highway outside Bon Accord. Not sure it was needed there at all. But I am no expert, I just expect the engineers to do better.

Another example is the San Fernando Bypass with four roundabouts in a two-mile stretch. If it wasn't for the well-designed Cross Crossing Interchange where a roundabout was moved, we would have had five in less than three miles.

I recently noticed two beautiful roundabouts within 50 metres of each other at the Debe end of the Solomon Hochoy Highway. Amazing technology. And there's the new stretch of roadway from Curepe to Kelly Village looking resplendent with its own share of twin roundabouts within a few metres of each other.

Roundabouts by the Chaguanas overpass to PriceSmart puts you through the torture of driving north to one roundabout, then south to another. There is even a roundabout at the end of the highway to Point Fortin. I certainly hope that is temporary.

It seems that it's the simplest and most cost-effective way to regulate traffic flow or to redirect it. Such is the case with the third roundabout near Tarouba, where another one was added as a major turn-off to the highway.

We certainly didn't need another roundabout there. It is a nightmare to negotiate there at any time of the day. It tests your nerves, reduces your energy and increases your stress, and it affects our productivity and the nation's progress.

While there is nothing essentially wrong with a roundabout, one must admit there is room for consideration in constructing alternative access configurations, to ensure safety at major intersections.

Throughout history, we have often found that the prevailing technology may not be the best option, even though the experts say so. Let's think again, engineers.

I may have used the word roundabout in this letter too many times, circumlocution one might say. But then again isn't that a reflection of the increasing number of roundabouts we have in the country?

On the other hand, it is hoped the Government would handle the issues of the country in a more direct manner, than the old roundabout way we are used to getting things done.

'BOTANIC GARDENS' IN SOUTH NEEDS CARE

NEWSDAY

Friday, 2nd December 2016

THE EDITOR:

But this evergreen vista holds a secret. It has been aptly described as the second "botanic gardens" of TT. It was John Cyril Augustus, then curator of the Royal Botanic Gardens in Port-of-Spain, who journeyed to the south to manage the Palmiste Estate and created Palmiste Park.

I recently came across a speech by Sir Norman Lamont in his book 'Problems in Trinidad', published in 1933. As the owner of Palmiste Estate, he acknowledged the assistance of Mr. and Mrs. Augustus and his hard-working gardener Persaddi, in developing the garden.

Today, the south "botanic gardens" waits to be rediscovered. It needs to be cared for and curated.

While we are all aware of the Botanic Gardens in Port-of-Spain, there is a poignant and forgotten fact that south Trinidad has its own veritable botanical arrangement.

For those who have not ventured south, the area is picturesque with grand old trees with tortuous rooted trees and nearby evergreen foliage, amid landscaped open patches of green. It gives a refreshing and even therapeutic relief to many who venture for exercise, picnic, or an afternoon stroll.

The area boasts trees from faraway countries. There is even a pistachio tree standing proudly, unnoticed at the side of the roadway that traverses a section of the park.

Old identification signs, now faded, tell the story of the botanical name and fame of the large imposing trees like "the devil's ear" that overshadow mortals as we walk beneath its spreading branches along the shaded path.

Squirrels scamper from tree to tree and lizards play in the afternoon sun in a community teeming with life. Then there's the old giant silk cotton tree that still harbours the secrets of incantations, written on bits of paper and small dolls, hidden between its large buttress roots. And of course, there's the collection of proud Palmiste palms.

Many fell away in time but, like life, young eager trees are rising to take the place of the old and restore the sentinel collection that could be seen for many miles around.

Palmiste National Park is a revealing place; it speaks of our love for God and country. Yet, it remains our unheralded second major effort to prepare another Botanic Gardens in T&T.

But, while we commend the work of the maintenance groups that maintain its grounds, we must do more than just cut the grass. There must be new signs on the trees for children to appreciate the arboriculture and floriculture, we need to see the hibiscus and our national flowers bloom again, to be a living agriculture lesson for our youth.

Sadly, though, there are those among us who seem intent on spoiling the picture of pristine beauty, by littering and driving indiscriminately over the greens, while a few nearby residents encroach with impunity into its legal boundaries.

It's time to upgrade this heritage of the south, this lasting tribute to people who came before us. We must honour the heritage of this noble place and the work of those who have made this place an indelible part of the mosaic of life for the people in the south.

Let us hail our heritage and appreciate the beauty of the "botanic gardens" of the south at Palmiste National Park.

REQUIEM FOR THE GULF OF PARIA?

NEWSDAY

Tuesday, 25th August 2015

THE EDITOR:

Despite the frenzy of the election season, we need to keep alive some critical issues that require our ongoing attention.

One of them is the condition of the Gulf of Paria and the incidents of dead marine life that have washed ashore along the western coastline of the country. Seems like it's a forgotten issue, but the situation is grave.

In fact, one of the biggest crimes being perpetrated in TT is the pollution related to the death of both "big fish" and "small fry" in the Gulf. The recent reports of dwindling numbers of each catch by the fishermen and dead wildlife should be a concern to all.

This might very well be the requiem for the Gulf of Paria. The 3,000-square mile body of water is partially enclosed by the Northern Range and the southern tip of the country and provides a livelihood and recreation for many. It also presents the main shipping route for industrial operations and, unfortunately, other nefarious activities.

In the early days, the Indigenous people dived for pearls and fish. The Spanish colonizers named it Golfo de la Ballena (Gulf of the Whale), but the name was soon changed, after the extensive whaling operations. It later appeared on a later map as Golfo de Triste (Gulf of Sadness).

Interestingly, a town off the coastline of Venezuela bears that name. The English eventually named it Gulf of Paria. It would seem the Trinidadian version of the name today might well be "Gulf of Death" (Golfo de Muerto).

As I write, I am listening to the famous composition by Mozart, "Requiem Mass in D Minor". It seems a fitting tune to play for the Gulf of Paria, even for a documentary of sorts. It could be narrated, in part, by the deep-sea diver who once gave me a "mournful" description of a seabed with very little vegetation and sparse marine life.

Maybe it's not too late to save this beautiful body of water from adverse industrial activities and the "polluted lifestyles" of those who callously kill our marine life, and negatively affect the ecological balance of our environment.

Recently, I stood on the grounds of my alma mater, Naparima College, from its vantage point on the hill, and looked out to the open sea that has been an inspiration to many students of the illustrious institution. I wondered how well the placid surface of the Gulf of Paria seems to hide so many ills that have befallen it over the years.

In my youth, we fished in the Gulf and knew too well the mud and slush of the seabed that came to the shore.

During times of low tide, we sometimes walked up to 150 metres out to sea to hunt for sea crabs under the trunks of fallen coconut trees. Even then the darkened waters flowing by could not hide the oil-slicked banks of the rivers or the mass of debris that floated like small islands on the surface of the water.

As a nation we have progressed, but the price has been too costly. The gulf is a testament to the fact that we are destroying our environment. So, while we celebrate and spend the oil and gas money, the Gulf of Paria begs for mercy.

With all the pollutants entering the gulf from Point Lisas, Pointe-a-Pierre and Point Fortin, there seems little point in sharing this message. But we should all share in the commitment to make the gulf live again.

This situation certainly requires that all righteous thinking citizens should rise up and fulfil their God-given responsibility to preserve our country. The mandate given to us in the Garden of Eden was to accept responsibility for all living things on sea or land.

But, before we read the final rites, I believe we can resurrect the situation.

I challenge the Marine Institute, Environment Management Authority, and other agencies, to consider implementation of research studies on the life of the Gulf of Paria and seek to create restoration projects to bring renewed life to our favourite coastline.

So, with all the wrongs that have been perpetrated, we still have some time to make it right.

Let the Gulf of Paria live again.

MOB PURSUIT OF THE CJ JUST WILL NOT DO

NEWSDAY

Thursday, June 8th 2017

THE EDITOR:

We are not a nation given to resignations.

Time and time again we have been witnessed the numerous instances of people in public and private office being deemed guilty of actions, demeanours, and devious behaviour without the natural course of resignation from the public office they hold. The case of the Chief Justice is different. The throng calls for his resignation.

It is clearly a case that he who has the biggest stone should throw it.

The bacchanal and mauvais langue have so tainted our souls that we neither see the right nor seek the righteous path.

I stand in support of the Chief Justice.

I believe the system is indeed flawed and patently corrupted by the actions and intentions of the many who call for justice.

Lady justice grimaces as we pursue our pleasure. One of the main passions in our country is to devour each other.

We do not seem to lack the cunning, like a serial killer, to pursue our prey, the ones who try to follow after righteousness and stumble along the way.

One wonders then, who would have been standing if the stones were thrown at the last regime?

The follies of the leadership gave birth to such extreme deviations, that the proverbial mirror on the wall shattered, with the preponderance of truth that it spoke.

I write with a conviction that our nation needs to have a conscience that is nurtured by love, not the callous, uncaring pursuit of men of honour and distinction, who may or may not have faltered in their actions.

For those who call for justice in an untimely manner, having been "Rip van Winkles" and missed the real mess-ups of the previous government, I say check yourself.

Think again.

The folly of our efforts to implicate others is a characteristic cancer of our society that undermines the efforts of the few proponents of truth and justice among us.

So, some among us raise hands in mob-like madness, playing mas with our destiny, seeking to bring rectitude with an attitude that is taking us down the path of dishonesty to the town of despair.

I am truly troubled by the state of affairs.

For those who rise in comfort each day to do their dastardly acts, I say God does not sleep and what's good for the goose is good for the gander.

I pray that we will be able to achieve the true moral standard that our nation desires.

I am for truth and justice in the land, but this mob behaviour just will not do. Let those without sin cast the first stone. I rest my case.

COUNTRY NEEDS A PURGE, MR PM

NEWSDAY

Wednesday, 26 July 2017

THE EDITOR:

I was recently reminded how, as a child, I was given the usual "purge" during the August holidays. My excitement at the end of school and the start of "free time" with all its fun was tempered by my parents' wise move "to give the children a purge." Needless to say, it was a part of the holidays that kept me close to the bathroom for a while. The experience taught me that you can't have fun without doing the necessary cleansing of the innermost parts.

While some may challenge the activity as being unnecessary, there is a point to note that it served us quite well as children; if not just to slow us down and give us cause for reflection. Back then, it didn't matter how much you protested; our mothers knew best.

Today, I am of the view that our nation needs a purge. As we enter this period of our national history, we are pained by the constrictions to our progress, the serious financial constipation, moral decadence, and stomach-churning murders.

We have tried so many diets from the experts and naysayers, but there is some merit in applying the tried and tested occasional purge of our system, burdened as it is with a history of largesse and overindulgence.

I speak not of the routine call for a change in diet as administered by our political nutritionists, but a good doze of senna for the country, accompanied by a time for rest and reflection. This will definitely force us to sit down and contemplate our state.

We must challenge ourselves as a nation to do what is necessary, to reduce the harmful concoction of crime and moral decay, which are harmful to our consumption. Indeed, we must go deeper, beyond the dialogue and conversations to address the source of our malady and expel those elements that restrict us from operating efficiently.

We need to come clean with the reality of our situation before God and country, and set ourselves the task, though painful, to cleanse ourselves in body, soul, and spirit.

Although some among us have performed our religious duty of fasting and prayer, there is the urgent need for a national coordinated effort as a people to address the present state of our country.

I appeal to the Christian community, not to be content with a few days of prayer and fast, but to improve their regimen in addressing the spirits of crime, violence, and corruption, among others.

So, my call is for the "Christian collective" to join the rest of the nation in a special 40-day holy fast that would culminate with the expected freedoms on Independence Day and beyond.

At the beginning of this Government's term of office, I had called for a day of prayer and thanksgiving.

Now I am calling for a 40-day fast for the nation, a time of cleansing and a time when we can administer a "spiritual purge" to get rid of the undesirable elements that plague us. We have tried everything else, why not try the biblical method of securing guidance for a nation... "that the people would fast and pray, turn from their wicked ways and seek God" ...so that "a remnant will be blessed, and a nation will be purged of its sins." Time for our nation to take a "spiritual purge," Mr PM.

APOSTLE TERRENCE HONORE via email

SCHOLARS MUST DO RIGHT FOR GOD AND COUNTRY

NEWSDAY

Saturday, 24th October 20

THE EDITOR:

Indeed, they are now challenged to learn and make a difference.

Through their efforts, we can continue to reshape the economic landscape. They can study to enrich the true TT culture. It is of note that over the years, the number of scholarships has been increased from three to 443.

This is surely a sign of numerical growth and academic advancement, but it needs to be corroborated by empirical evidence of impact and growth in our nation state. Over time, many scholars have migrated to other shores, refusing to be part of the TT experience.

Others have absconded, while some scholars have hidden their brilliance under a "bushel". Sad, but true. Hopefully, this new group will have been conditioned differently, to prepare themselves to creatively address the myriad number of problems that we have to grapple with as an emerging nation.

Letters to the Editor

In the calypso "Portrait of Trinidad", the Mighty Sniper (Mervyn Hodge) sang, "...our scholars have sat and passed every test and put us right alongside the best." So, we have a legacy of brilliance, but yet simple solutions elude us, and we complicate things with our own brand of "commesse".

We tend to approach our situations like the proverbial "tar baby" of African folklore. Attempting to handle problems with the same old ways and means... getting ourselves into one sticky situation after another. Our efforts at governance are mostly characterised by foibles, faux pas, and fraudulence.

We seriously need more uncorrupted leaders, with sound values and a sense of service to country rather than self, as we seek to be the people, under the Caribbean sun, that God has destined us to be.

It is clear that TT does not need more "bright" people. We have plenty. What we need are people who would live right in the sight of God and make a positive contribution to the development of our country. What we really need is not just intelligence, but more common sense.

Even with the trump card of oil, gas, and the energy industry we appear unable to play the game and win. We seem to be on all fours trying to find a way out of the maddening economic maze.

Yet on reflection, our budgetary investments in education have not yielded a corresponding change in our socio-economic status. It is a challenge that our new scholars will have to seriously consider in pursuit of their respective fields of study.

Even so, one wonders if there is a correlation between the increase in white-collar crime and the number of scholars we have produced... but that is for another discussion.

So, scholars all, past and present, we need to utilise our uniqueness to influence positive change in our country and the world. We have to make scholarship and ingenuity a part of our day-to-day existence.

So herein lies the challenge, should our scholars choose to accept it. The morality graph is low, the economic graph fluctuating, the violence graph is rising, the energy graph is declining. It's now up to the scholars to learn to become true custodians of our culture. As scholars, they have to learn well and do right for God and country.

LET'S CELEBRATE UNITY OF TT

NEWSDAY

Thursday, 25th January 2018

THE EDITOR:

On January 1, 1889, the union of Trinidad and Tobago came into effect after some deliberation and pronouncement by the British parliament. This year marks the 119th anniversary of that historic event.

Through the years, not much has been made of the occasion. Some might consider it a marriage of convenience, as our children have been raised without an appreciation of the uniqueness of our relationship and the fact that we stayed together in the face of many attempts to divide us.

Some may even say it is destined that we go our separate ways, but the fact remains that when the "I do" was announced in 1899, it was for the long haul. We have stayed together.

We must celebrate our connection that has survived a generation of agitation and bickering. Like a marriage, there have been the quarrels, the call for separate governance, while our children look on in dismay.

I dare say that the generation today is still as committed to the uniqueness of the "Trinbago" culture as reflected in our festivals and activities. There are no goat and crab races in Trinidad or any vibrant fervent cultural mix in Tobago, but we remain a good blend. We are distinct, but not apart, the uniqueness of a nation that is two, yet one.

Or is it that we can stand alone? Why haven't our brilliant minds determined a way for self-government or some other form of existence, which satisfies the purists among us?

Maybe, somewhere in a backroom or on a street corner, some of us quietly long for being truly Tobagonian or Trinidadian and not being annexed as a nation, but that remains a distant possibility. And as calypsonian Spoiler sang, "Trinidad and Tobago will always be one."

We both ended our relationships with our British colonisers; a people once enamoured by the queen and crown, who sang to the Union Jack like a mantra; learned to appreciate the sweet strains of our national anthem, and rose to thank God for the red, white, and black that flutters so proudly in the breeze.

And so, our independence from colonial control in 1962 gave us the right to be free, to determine our own destiny and we journeyed on, hand in hand, to become a twin-island republic in 1976. Today our relationship remains strong.

We moved on as a nation... we left the colonial relationship to embrace one love. And so, we are in this together, to aspire and achieve. Ours is a relationship of love and duty, a shared responsibility to survive and excel in our endeavours.

While there may be imaginary lines of distinction like south from north Trinidad, or the separating sea from Scarborough to Toco, we remain resolute in our efforts to keep the "marriage alive."

Regrettably, we have grown accustomed to not having seen any celebration about the union of Trinidad and Tobago or any recognition of what occurred in January 1899. Like much of our history, it has been discarded and destroyed by callous custodians and a people who fete away their ethos without much reflection and appreciation for our past, and the knowledge that guides our destiny.

Not another holiday certainly, but we can definitely recognise and celebrate the union of our beautiful islands, the reality that we remain one nation under God.

We draw from the words of the song "God Bless our Nation" as written by Marjorie Padmore: "May we possess the common love/ That binds and makes us one /...We can boast of unity / And take a pride in our liberty."

Now is the appointed time to plan and organise even the simplest of events honouring the anniversary of our unitary State. Reminding ourselves and educating our children on the intrinsic beauty of TT — our unity.

I stand in awe of what God has done in keeping our country in one "house" and not giving in to the ill-advised lure of going our separate ways.

What God has joined together, let no man try to put asunder.

PRAISE FOR POLICE ACTION

NEWSDAY

Thursday, 25th January 2018

THE EDITOR:

The recent incident of an attempted larceny of items from the San Fernando Nazarene Church, and the swift response of the police officers should not go by without comment.

The officers involved must be commended for their role in capturing the perpetrators. It was an act of God. The church in question and the Christian community in general, must be grateful for the timely action of the police.

An act of sacrilege such as was reported is symptomatic of the times in which we live, the lawlessness reveals a lack of spiritual consciousness that has given rise to devious actions and heinous crimes in our society.

The recent incident reminds us that not even the church is outside of the grasp of the criminal element. Indeed, we all have to be more sober and vigilant in these times that continue to try men's souls.

The timely intervention of members of the fraud squad as reported, gives us some hope and comfort that our efforts are not in vain. While the church continues to pray, we encourage the police to continue to do their duty in protecting us all.

While we acknowledge the role of the police service in protecting and serving our community, we must also admonish the churches to continue to provide much needed spiritual care to the people of our country. We are partners in crime prevention.

So, there is need for further collaboration between the police in the execution of their duties and the church in its role and function. Increased opportunities for prayer with the police and encouraging the officers to pray before going out on duty, are two ways that the church can be of greater assistance.

In a previous letter to the Commissioner, I requested that an opportunity be given for Ministers of religion to partner with police in crime prevention. I reiterate that this must be considered as a reasonable option given the state of crime in the country.

While new collaborative methods must be used, they must be complemented by proven and tested measures, like prayer and counselling, as we treat with the increase in criminal acts.

Other measures can include restoring the Mentoring Program and various community-based initiatives that will serve to support the work of the police service. The church has remained committed to this task.

And so, we praise the police for their action and recognize their efficiency in this matter, but we must continue to work collaboratively to effectively address crime in our country.

A HIGHWAY FOR HASELY

NEWSDAY
Saturday, 28th July 2018

THE EDITOR:

July 24th marked the anniversary of the day that Hasely Crawford won our nation's first Olympic gold medal in Montreal.

Now, 42 years after his historic achievement, the people of the city of San Fernando are yet to see a sign, a plaque, or even a statue in his honour.

Over the years, many great ideas have been considered, and there was even an exhibition on his 40th anniversary in 2017, organised by University of the West Indies and the National Gas Company.

But what will be more fitting is to have a permanent public honour, such as the renaming of the roadway from Marabella to Mosquito Creek as the Hasely Crawford Highway.

No side street or street corner sign would do for this champion of the soil.

The 13.1 kilometre "highway" will extend from the Marabella roundabout, through the San Fernando Bypass, all the way to the Mosquito Creek boundary of the city of San Fernando. This includes the section of roadway that was recently paved and looks ready for a good name.

Indeed, the roadways deserve better names than the South Trunk Road or the San Fernando Bypass. The former reflects the old title for major roadways under the British system, while the bypass, built in the 1940s, is no longer a valid name as the road now bisects the city.

Interestingly, the English Cambridge Dictionary defines the Trunk Road as "an important road for travelling long distances at high speed." How appropriate and definitive, it's a Hasely Crawford-type road.

The fact that he was born in the city of San Fernando, is a good argument for placing an attractive highway sign with his name in the vicinity.

Crawford was among some outstanding sportsmen who came from the community, along with the likes of Mansingh Amarsingh (table tennis) and Raphick Jumadeen (cricket), among others.

But it was Crawford who got Olympic gold. We have to give honour to whom honour is due, according to the Bible (Romans 13:7b) – even belatedly.

Today, Crawford deserves a recognition befitting his golden achievement. He is our sports royalty, a true son of the soil – of the south.

TIME TO GO TO CHURCH

NEWSDAY

Friday, 17th August 2018

THE EDITOR:

Notwithstanding the context of the recent utterance by the Prime Minister, that a certain individual should go to "church," it still stands as one of the most profound statements that he has made during his time in office.

I totally concur with him. There is an urgent need for people to go to church, to find a place of worship and to seek God, especially in times like this. Going to church is not a diversion from the routine, or just a penance for the erring soul, but an essential part of the fabric of our society, which has become tattered and torn over the years.

There has been a falling away. People in our country prefer to 'play instead of pray'. The cry "Oh God!" comes often at the time of last resort, when all else seems to be lost. Such is the state of affairs in our country that we must go back to basics. Returning to the times when the church was a vital and integral part of the lives of our people and church attendance was the norm in our communities.

Those were the days when the family went to church together, when there was time to recognise that God is in the midst of each situation. We have been "wining away" or spirituality. "Dissing" God and devaluing the time set aside for worship. We are a nation in distress because we are a nation in a mess.

For many, going to church is not in style. It seems like it's not cool to gather for prayer. People seem to have no time for that. But it's not too late to stem the tide of crime and moral decay in our society if we would only pray and act on our prayers. This requires that we pray both in our private time, "our closet," as the Bible says, and in public, where people are gathered to pray and to praise God. I look to the day when public prayer is more popular. But for now, we just need to get back to church, as advised by the Prime Minister. The option is both timely and relevant to our needs.

Going to church implies that we are ready and willing to go to God, and to recognise our shortcomings, even among those in the assembly of the righteous.

Yes, it is important for the PM to let the nation know that our relationship with God is central to the success of our country. We have to stop being frivolous about that relationship with God and go to church.

We must not just go to church for tradition, but as a soul solution for our nation. To deal with crime, corruption, physical abuse and all the other ills of our society, we must take the sound advice that is echoed in the Bible and simply go to church – i.e., not to forsake the gathering of yourselves.

Historically, we moved from no business on Sunday, no selling of liquor etc, to a total disregard for the holy day. We have gone astray, and no amount of legislation could put us right. It is holiness that will exalt our nation, not political persuasion or a Sunday beach lime. When will we wake up and see that "is we who killing we"?

Pausing for prayer and finding a place of worship is a positive force for the stability of our nation. The PM was "pointed" in his pronouncement but let us be "general" to say Trinidadians and Tobagonians must go back to church.

It is clear that any group of people with a shared common interest will gather together – as simple as it sounds. Christians should gather, go to church, just because they are Christians and followers of Jesus Christ.

Let's use this opportunity to encourage all people to go to Church – to pray and to worship for the sake of our souls and for our nation. This is truly an admonition to save our nation. Thank you, Mr PM.

LET'S CARE FOR THE CAREGIVERS

NEWSDAY

Saturday, 19th May 2018

THE EDITOR:

The recent untimely passing of the medical doctor attached to St. Ann's Hospital and the idea that he might have committed suicide is an uncomfortable thought, especially for the thousands of individuals who work to provide healthcare to our nation.

The incident pointedly raises questions about the health and well-being of those who provide care to patients in need.

While we are not yet fully aware of the details of this unfortunate incident, we are made painfully aware of the need for a review of the care being provided for all staff at our health institutions.

Several years ago, I was shocked to learn that medical organisations did not provide a programme of support and assistance for members of staff, including medical doctors, who give of their substance in performing their duties.

I found it ironic, that an organisation that provided care for others, seemed to be failing in its responsibilities to provide care for its caregivers.

I am advocating for the establishment of employee assistance programmes and peer support programmes in the health sector. Also, consideration should be given to ensuring that annual health screening should be part of the package of employment. No health care worker should be denied personal health screening and professional care.

I shuddered when I saw health care workers standing in long lines, drawn away from their jobs due to illness, but unable to return in a timely manner to serve the very people they were standing with.

I also saw situations where medical health sick bays and sick rooms were not adequately furnished, to provide care for medical personnel as part of a wellness programme.

I know what it's like to have to console doctors after tough clinic sessions, or comfort nurses who work double shifts and different postings; to hear of their personal problems that weigh heavily on their minds. They are human too.

I am calling for the Minister of Health to institute a mandatory review of the health care provisions for members of the medical fraternity and implement measures to ensure that hospital staff receive medical attention on a timely basis.

We must ensure that all medical personnel receive the care they need when needed.

This situation begs the question: how can health care professionals provide care for the patients if they don't get care for themselves? Working as they do under adverse conditions, with limited access to personal health care, is a cause for high stress, ill health, and unforeseen circumstances among health care workers.

Whatever the precipitating factors leading to the death of the young doctor, the incident compels us to beseech the Minister of Health to address this matter post-haste.

I pray that something is done about this situation. Let's care for those who care Mr Minister.

CHRISTMAS IS FOR CHRISTIANS

NEWSDAY

Thursday, 13th December 2018

THE EDITOR:

At the risk of sounding redundant, I emphatically state that the season of Christmas is distinctly a Christian event. It seems that we need to remind all and sundry that Christmas is for Christians.

There are celebrations for the different religious groups in our lovely rainbow society, but this must reflect distinctiveness, not inclusiveness. For while we respect and accommodate each other, there is need for us to appreciate and respect the differences.

Over the years, there seems to have been a merging of the views and values among streams of religious practice. Many point to the assimilation that historically occurred in the Siparia community – with a shared festival for Christians and non-Christians – but that should be considered an anomaly rather than a norm.

The uniqueness of each faith must be maintained in spite of the proximity, and affinity that goes with living in the same community and breathing the same air.

Beyond that, there is a spiritual orientation that dictates that we maintain the purity and integrity of our different faiths.

While I recognise the diverse religious practices that have become a part of our cultural landscape, we need to respect the core spiritual ideals of the religions that make up our society. To do differently is to compromise the very essence of our existence as followers of different faiths.

The Christmas season comes as the last religious event for the calendar year, bringing with it the elements that are revered by Christians and respected by people of other religions.

But it is worth reminding Christians that we must maintain the purity of the purpose of the season, in celebrating the birth of our lord and saviour Jesus Christ.

The secularisation of this sacred season and the distortions of the truth regarding the significance of Christmas Day, have clouded the real purpose of the occasion. To really celebrate Christmas is to know Christ.

Many have sung songs to "put Christ in our Christmas" amid the many festive renderings of parang and other forms of felicitous songs. The removal of Christ in Christmas results in plain "old mas."

But it's not about going back to the real reason for the season as many chose to say. It is not Christmas which has left us, it is we who have left the meaning of the season behind, in our effort to share and share alike and to emphasise the festivity and not the nativity.

So, it's a reminder to us all that this sacred season is about Jesus Christ and not only about the business bargains. Discounts may be nice, but we cannot devalue Christmas to mere currency of coins and dollars. Instead, we must embrace the utility of Christmas time, as true Christians should and do.

While a few among us choose not to celebrate the season, it remains as it is – a recollection of the genesis of the salvation of mankind.

The true worth of the season is to celebrate the birth of our lord and saviour Jesus Christ. Let all Christians arise and be true to this declaration.

Let us do the duty and live and love as the true message of the season. As a Christian, a follower of Jesus Christ, I am calling it as it is. Christmas is for Christians. Let's endeavour to keep it so.

SOUTH CHURCHES READY TO SUPPORT LAID-OFF WORKERS

NEWSDAY

Friday, 7th December 2018

THE EDITOR:

The Christian Council of San Fernando expresses its concern and support for the many affected by the recent layoffs and terminations of employment at Petrotrin and TSTT.

To our dear brothers and sisters – members of the affected families – we who are bonded by our shared experiences of having worked in the oil and service industry in contributing to the development of our nation, we wish to advise you that the Christian church is ready and willing to provide spiritual support in these trying times.

We are indeed committed to your cause and cognisant of the impact that the closure of the Pointe-a-Pierre refinery and other services have on our communities. We give you the assurance that we stand with you in these testing times.

Let us have faith in the providence of God. We join you in asking for God's divine intervention and pray for His guidance as we move forward.

We pray that God will grant you the wisdom and increased faith to achieve a sense of hope in these dark days.

As the church, we are committed to providing you with prayerful support at this time and into the future.

As in the days when sugar died or when Caroni closed and other enterprises folded, we know that God will make a way for us as a people and as a nation.

Be encouraged. Please contact your nearest clergyman for guidance and counsel. May God continue to bless us all.

Some of the participating churches include Voice of Triumph (Rev Trevor Joefield), Seventh Day Adventist Cocoyea (Rev Codelle Williams), St Paul's Anglican Church (Fr Anthony Mowlah Baksh), Christ Exalted Ministries (Apostle Wayne Bedeau), Rochard Worship Centre (Rev Terrence Chapman), Zion Tabernacle (Apostle Masceline Wyatt), and Susamachar Presbyterian Church (Rev Kendrick Sooknarine).

Our Lady of Perpetual Help (Fr David Khan), Salvation Army (Rev. Neyere Moliere), San Fernando Methodist (Rev. Dwayne Samm), and the Christian Council of San Fernando (Apostle Terrence Honore, chairman).

The council was established in January to consider the spiritual well-being of San Fernando and the nation.

APOSTLE TERRENCE HONORE
Christian Council of San Fernando

STAY UP, MR COMMISSIONER

NEWSDAY

Sunday, 13th January 2019

THE EDITOR:

We are doing it again. The recent attack on the Commissioner of Police's "one shot, one kill" approach is typical of the way people in TT treat with any attempt to correct the wrongs and raise the rights.

It is a pathetic pastime that needs serious prayers.

There is a learned inclination to pull down anything that appears to be good and anybody trying to do good.

I make no apology for this analysis of our situation and my concern with those who express the view that "one shot, one kill" is an undesirable position for the police to adopt. What is the alternative? What is the prescribed solution for a nation facing a crisis of crime?

While we should not condone unjustified killing by the police, we certainly cannot support the galloping murder rate. We will be like "mules and fools" if we do.

As the Bible says, "I will instruct you and teach you the way you should go; I will give you counsel and watch over you. Do not be like the horse or mule, which have no understanding; they must be controlled with bit and bridle to make them come to you" (Psalm 32:8,9).

It's passing strange that when we try to address a problem in our society the naysayers and pontificators bring their old talk to the "gayelle" while bodies pile up, and mothers hold their bellies and bawl. Some of us question the resolution to the problem and seem to champion the status quo.

If it sounds good, 'bad talk' it. If it looks clean, litter it. If the top cop is starting to get results, criticise him. Like the old calypsonian sang, it seems "we like it so."

How else can we explain the logic of people joining with the criminals to attack the CoP. It's a dastardly attempt to stay in the "comfort of the crime." All this bad attitude is the cause of crime and violence in our midst.

And so, we created a "criminal state" and a country littered with garbage and woes, and some are unashamedly trying to destroy attempts to correct our wrongs. Even while many among us cry out in pain, others shout out in disdain, attacking all that is right, and good and true.

We seem to be unwilling or unable to address the monster in our midst, the same one that we have raised in our communities. Like the Bible story there is a need for a David to tackle the Goliath and reduce crime. But the brothers don't want that. The commissioner is trying his "sling and thing" to bring down the crime, but others are trying to hold him back and pull him down.

So, we will pray for the police and all law-abiding citizens who are in shock at the state of our nation.

Many of our citizens feel helpless against the crime and criminal activity. Some have come to accept it as the norm. But there is a God above and He will raise up heroes in our time to tackle the scourge of crime and rescue our country. Blessed is the nation whose God is the Lord.

Marvel not that I say unto you, we need to be "born again" in our thinking and turn to God for the salvation of our nation.

We must fight crime on the beaches, we must fight crime on the hills, we must fight crime in the streets of every town and village and we must not surrender. We must continue the fight against the forces of evil.

For all of us, who are fighting to bring down crime, I say stay up, Mr Commissioner. You are doing a good job. Don't come down.

COMMENTARY

CHRISTIANS AND CARNIVAL

NEWSDAY

Tuesday, 5th March 2019

THE EDITOR:

Christians seem to have no answer to carnival, so why preach against it when you can't change it? That's the question that has been asked since back in the days of Noah… so the Bible says.

For many among us, it's folly not to follow all the wining and jamming on Carnival days.

It's a moot point to try to persuade people to stop the carnival. The thought causes people to set up like "jack Spaniard" when anyone says something 'off key' about the good time they have enjoying the music of the carnival season.

It is ludicrous to say the least, to engage a wirebender, costume maker or masquerade in a conversation while the wining is on their mind. 'Nobody could stop this carnival' has been a chant for years. Even an erring English clergyman joined the revelry, so calypsonian the Mighty Cypher had to sing, 'If the priest could play who is we.'

So, why try to change the minds of people… Join them in the revelry. But that's a conundrum for the Christian who has grown up in the bacchanal that is Carnival. We grew up knowing the three seasons of our Trinidad and Tobago… dry season, wet season, and carnival season.

It's hard to be in it and not part of it. The beat is infectious, the rhythm almost divine, orchestrated by a master composer of the heavenly vintage. The crafts of calypso and soca, mixed with the steelband, is a heady concoction even for the stout of heart.

Many have tried but failed to separate themselves from the festivity that has become our nation's trademark and apparent destiny. 'Come wine with we' is the 'tourism' call to all who dare to look our way. The music draws you in... it's hard to miss the beat you have been hearing since you were born. We are truly a nation with a mix of people of fete and people of faith.

And so, Carnival goes on, the much-heralded artistry and vocalizations, wining and gyrations in a melee that mesmerizes the mind and takes pleasure to giddy heights, with people "mashing up" the place for a week. The radio stations changing their tunes just for the season, as people crave for the popular songs and the streets become a theatre with prancing and dancing hordes of worshipers of Bacchus.

Meanwhile, the Christians beat a hasty retreat to the beaches and far reaches of the hills and coastline. Just to stay pure by the seashore, but the whole island seems to be pulsating with the rhythm of carnival. It's a long-time thing, going on long before we were born. Others choose the quiet side of the carnival season, but it's hard to escape the beat. To some it is gladness.... for others it is madness.

Meanwhile, gifted songsters challenge each other for first place, in a growing range of high-octane song contests and masquerade parades. And the nation changes its political status to become a monarchy if not just for a weekend, when the kings and queens come forth, from almost every school, village, and town, parading in their splendour. Royalty for a day they say.

Many parade the festive spirit with pride, and with all the pomp and circumstance, in a mockery of the monarchy of yesteryear. And the children come out in tow...learning to wine and step in time, but they can't reach Sunday school with the same vigour and zest.

So, this is carnival... drunken men lying in the carnal, overcome by rum and the rhythm of the music. Scantily clad ladies daring all to see as much of their 'birthday suit' as can be seen, all proud of their anatomy glittering in the noon day sun. Who could show more breast is the test? And the 'puritan' Christian frowns on.

The festivity seems unchallenged as the most celebrated time of the year. It's the national days when people come out to play, to release the pressure and vocalize all the vapid arguments made to justify the wantonness and even jamette behaviour. But that is the view of a few Church people if you will. Others have long joined the wining hordes in gay revelry and abandon of their personal pride...nothing to hide. God could join 'we too'.

And the beat goes on. People hear different sounds at carnival time, each to his own rhythm and rhyme. But does it lift us to world class heights? We seem to have lost the steel pan to others, our masqueraders are certainly matched by those of other countries, but our sheer tenacity to maintain the revelry with remain, proudly displayed by a flag woman or man prancing in a street parade as the banners sway on in the morning breeze.

So, we see masquerades mesmerised by the music and moving in time to the conductor's hand. And people 'catching the power 'dancing with glee in the unbridled festivity. That is carnival, a cultic melee, where people worship with their hips and lips and not their heart.

But everything has a season, and everything has its place. Some people say carnival is here to stay. Preach or pray, people will find pleasure and leisure in the season. So, the spirit of carnival reigns like many other spirits that roam and rule in our land. Let Christians to do what they are called to do.... pray for the souls of men.

What's interesting is for Christians to see how people jumping up as one...the sense of commitment and fun in the sun. We are yet to see that in Christianity with its many bands and brands listening to the same sacred tune but dancing out of God's timing.

Then will come lent. People pious, with ashen faces, all creeds and races, trying to wash away the sin that stained their skin but their heart longs for the beat to go on. To many …next year Carnival here already.

So, taxpayers pay to play... the coffers of the state offers the way, to fete for a day and 'dingolay'. What can a Christian say? Some have changed their style of worship and song, redeemed from the pleasures of the pastime. The masses continue to worship in the Carnival way. But the Christian wouldn't let Bacchus be God, not even for a day.

Christians can't understand why people play themselves so much at carnival... but the culture done mix, the maestro has his tricks, to get even the faithful in heart to play their part, in the carnival culture.

Many people will continue to say, the carnival mentality will have its sway... shaping the minds and hearts of the people, caressing our culture with its smooth and sultry movements, its artistry and grand theatre.

We in the carnival, the carnival in we… it is shaping the nation's destiny with the Christians in the minority.

What is to be will be... 'but God eh done with we'

So, Carnival people play on while the Christians pray on.

LET'S RESPECT OUR HOLY DAYS

NEWSDAY

Thursday, 13th June 2019

THE EDITOR:

There are 14 days assigned as public holidays in our country. Seven of these are ceremonial, like Independence Day and Republic Day, while the other seven should be more accurately referred to as holy days.

The issue is not in the number of holidays, but in the way we treat our holy days. While all holidays – days of commemoration – should be respected, the holy days – set aside for religious observances – should be revered and protected.

One of the indicators of a healthy nation is how we treat our sacred days. New social strategies and other measures are inadequate in themselves to sustain us as a nation, but our holy days must be well kept, as we seek to preserve our values. Our felicity has encroached on our spirituality.

Although many faithful still practise their respective religions, there is a creeping sense of dissociation with the holiness of our sacred days, as distinct from holidays or ceremonial days and other observances. This is not a good sign for a fledgling nation, as hedonism and materialism seem to be having sway on the way we treat our holy days.

I checked the etymology and found that the English did that to us, like so many other things. They set us up with rhyme with no reason, and we are holding on to it, without considering how the change in the appellation is affecting our nation. The word "holiday" is rooted in an old English word, haligdæg (halig "holy" + dæg "day"), used in reference to special religious days; but over the years it has morphed to become a special day of rest or relaxation, a time to stay away from work or school.

So, the name of the day for religious observances changed in meaning, with one letter from a day of piety to one of festivity.

Our deep-set desire to revel, emanating from our freedom from slavery and indentureship, has shaped our attitude to all things, including that of our holy days. But it remains that the true strength of our people is in our spirituality. We should not treat it with frivolity and pursue pleasure only as the main course for our nation.

Yes, we are a festive, fun-loving people but maybe we have failed to see the subtle changes that our preoccupation with pleasure has had on our religious persuasion and ultimately our values.

We are becoming a people who seem to care less about the spiritual ideals that holy days represent. Our value standards are falling, the rum and fete are calling, and the nation seems drunk with pursuing pleasure and leisure instead of keeping the faith.

The sacred and the sanctified are being cast aside. Holy day or holiday, some people still "come out to play." All things have become equal in our insatiable appetite for fete. The significance of the religious seasons has become less conspicuous, and we are producing more limers than worshippers.

Now the children are rising up to be "just like we." A people who parties more than they praise, a nation that finds its pleasure in more holidays and disregards the significance of holy days. We are throwing parties in Lent and desecrating our worship days and making our holy days a time to lime. It is to our detriment.

Let's keep our spiritual ideals in their rightful place. Let's treat our holy days as more than just holidays, so we can change our ways and save our nation.

LETTERS TO THE EDITOR

DO AWAY WITH SEA SIN

NEWSDAY

Monday, 1st July 2019

THE EDITOR:

The Ministry of Education needs to address the mental torture of the children of our nation with the current SEA examination. We need to consider the depth of despair that the nation has to bear, with the continuance of this dreaded form of assessment. The wilful and deliberate subjection of our children and parents to the rigours of the SEA is nothing short of a sinful act... doing deliberate harm to our children.

A sin my brothers, is a thought or an act that intentionally or unintentionally does harm to another human being in the sight of God. The SEA examination is an abomination to the nation. I am praying for the cessation of this insensitive form of assessment that has scared the society through the years of its existence. We must do better.

Many voices have risen over the years and even louder in recent times... to do away with the SEA and allow the nation to breath. But who is listening? There is no discounting the numerous casualties as a consequence of the SEA: the low self-esteem, the despondency, the lack of hope and even, in some instances, degeneration to a life of crime.

The authorities need to 'repent' for the suffering experienced by the individuals who struggle through the year of preparation. The situation has risen to high heavens.

Today, hundreds of children cry uncontrollably after not getting their 'first' or 'second' choice selection. What an indictment of our nation's education system. And some of us just stand by and watch the children cry.

We have to console so many parents and children after the announcements of the results. Then there are the perpetual arguments about the prestige and non-prestige school placements.

What we are embracing in our bosom, is a contravention of the natural law of progression, for our aspiring scholars and the lack of a reasonable and fair opportunity for advancement in the world.

I am compelled to ask the dreaded question... why is SEA still a part of the education system? Any reasonable person will appreciate the damage being done and the long-term effects of this system... one that has evolved over the years, into a virtual monster in our midst.

Our leaders need to heed the call... hear the cries. This behemoth of our education system must fall. Down with the SEA!.. up with a modern, more practical assessment system. May God help us all in righting this wrong!

COMMENTARY

LET'S STAND WITH THE MEN IN BLUE

NEWSDAY

Wednesday, 30th October 2019

WE HAIL the recent acquisition of the Pointe-a-Pierre refinery by the Oilfields Workers Trade Union (OWTU) as a milestone in the history of our country. It's a long time coming from the days of the barefoot "warriors" in the muddy tracks of the early oilfields. It's like a big oil find of yesteryear.

It was the toil in the oil that shaped our land and gave energy and growth to our beautiful country. Our economic history is intertwined with that of the emergence and rise of the OWTU. It's an institution that has stood against the tyranny of the past, the bastions of imperialism and the exploitation of our resources and our people. It fought to promote our dignity and preserve our land. Now it stands with this new acquisition in hand.

The next stage of our journey is being championed by those men and women who have held the reins of labour for these many years, as it is said, through blood, sweat and tears. The tables have turned, and now the OWTU sits on the other side, to bargain for effective management of our refinery and to represent members of the working class. We stand with you.

But there is no magic wand to the restoration of the energy sector, after years of decline. The OWTU has played its role well on the national stage, not giving an inch to those who have sought to exploit our little island, big with oil and gas. The power has shifted hands, like a chess game of eminent proportions; the fortunes of the oil industry now favour the brave, those who stood in the rain and made the call – forward ever, backward never.

We saw the chimney stacks of the sugar cane industry fall and give way to the oil refinery with its silvery columns of steel, now glittering hopefully in the sun. They stand like silent sentinels to our past, now awaiting their day of liberation. The refinery needed a saviour.

It has always been a bread-and-butter issue, all about survival of our economy, of our country. Ours is a culture derived from oil exploits and largely deprived from sharing in the wealth and success in a meaningful way. The countryside looks sad, with towns like Fyzabad still waiting on their redemption. And the man in the market waits for an intervention, while the eager child seeks to secure the future in his school bag.

The OWTU can work to change this situation. It has to rise to another challenge, but that has been its nature. Many have tried to court the warriors of the OWTU, fete them or persuade them, but they must remain true to the ideals of trade unionism – to stand for the rights of the downtrodden, the poor and the needy. It's biblical in its scope and intent. The preachy posture was indeed adopted by the first leader, Uriah "Buzz" Butler, in righting the wrongs for the working class.

But it's of concern to note that some people are standing on the sidelines, looking on with cynicism at the proverbial "loud-mouth" union men, who struck fear in the hearts of the white colour class with their blue shirts and powerful lyrics.

The OWTU has achieved its long-touted goals; it has overcome, even taken control, to stand as a giant in the land.

The men and women of the OWTU are now set to preserve our heritage and protect our national interest from the marauding sharks of the economic order.

And so, we march on with the men in blue. Now that labour indeed holds the reins. Our country needs this group of hardy warriors to marshal their forces, and to raise the banners of hope and prosperity.

We herald the spirit of those who have gone before, the many who stood up for "bread, peace and justice" to ensure the economic health and well-being of the people of TT.

It is well known that the Christian church has always stood with the men in blue as they sang the old gospel song "We shall overcome. We shall overcome someday," an anthem that merged with the silent prayers of concerned wives and children. God has heard the cries and deep in our hearts we do believe, you have overcome.

To the other heroes of our land, who never received a national award, the men who toiled in the mud and late into the night, who prayed to God for "betterment" and for a fair day's pay for a fair day's work, your time has come.

Now we can see the old heroes of the early oil days, sitting on their favourite chairs and chanting quietly into the night. Massa day now done! Let's stand with the men in blue!

COMMENTARY

BARING THE TRUTH

NEWSDAY

Friday, 8th November 2019

THE EDITOR:

THE RECENT incident of scantily clad models parading in the sanctity of the Anglican cathedral, laid bare the issue of disrespect for the norms and standards of Christianity. This behaviour reflects the tastes and interests of some people in TT – reveal your body and to hell with holiness.

But I prefer to look at it not from eye level, as tempting as that may be, but from the bird's eye view of this occurrence. This episode has a greater significance for the church in a nation that has embraced partial nudity, and exposure of the human form in a vulgar way.

Years ago, the priest took to the streets to play mas. "If the priest could play who is me," sang the calypsonian. Today, the mas took to the aisle of the church to return the favour and promote something of a different flavour, that the parishioners have only been accustomed to seeing on the streets.

While there is shock and awe at the audacity of the designers to portray their creative outfits in the church – as they have been doing over the years in this Carnival crazy nation – it's really nothing new, in a sense. We are long past our innocence as a people for propriety and dignity and purity. The devil is in the details.

The portrayal revealed the bare facts, the true nature of things. We are far along the road to nudity in public places, and we can't deny that the church reflects the preferences, interests, and pastimes of the people of TT. After all, we live here.

Women now worship with no head covering and in sleeveless dress and jeans. But some people are trying to be holy and maintain at least a spot where sanctity exists. This is really about models behaving unruly in a holy place. This must be at least a crime of disorderly conduct or disturbing the peace of God.

But many would agree that there should be a repository or remnant of sanctity that should not be trifled with and crossing it would bring the ire of God. Whose God?... a reveller would ask. The same God who said that revelry is a sin and wanton behaviour is unacceptable, especially the painted bodies, the skimpy outfits, and the G-string designs. But that's what some people crave.

We are in a dental floss culture of apparel, and its apparent that the people who promote chastity and decency are blind to the fact that the no-clothes boundary was crossed many years ago.

We are a nation on the loose. Nobody can stop our behaviour; it's total disorder. Bacchus reigns and the clothes lines are thin on the skin. Pleasure to the eye for the passer-by, especially at Carnival time, when people 'wine pass' the churches and wonder when they would get in to mash up the place.

The dastardly deed has been done. The fashion show exposed our lack of purity but revealed in some minds the release of inhibitions that the church holds up against a breakaway society.

One couldn't help but notice the national colours being well displayed, patriotic and vitriolic in their content and candour, the designs vivid and dramatic, the colours bold and unashamed. This is where we are as a nation. It's a wake-up call to the cultural divide of our country. We are in a mess. No, we are in mas, the Carnival type, all year round.

But many wouldn't see it the same way. The old standards are falling. The beach is the canvas of how far we have come. The streets are our theatres and now the church feels the pressure of a culture that has run amok of all that is decent to the God-fearing, while others try to keep the true standards as their duty to society.

What can I say to my Christian brothers? I remember the days when cinema was sin, when the television was a tool of the enemy, and it was a popular theme of the Sunday sermon. That changed when the skirt lines went higher and bust lines came lower and, worse, the swimwear got skimpier, as the models showed off for all to see. So, things have changed, we have to deal with it.

No, the church aisle is not a runway, but we must be real in what we say to the people, to the world, in the face of God and on the streets and in public places. God is not only in our walled places of worship. You can't disrespect Him outside and be holy inside. God forbid. We cannot accept and condone on the street and not expect it to enter the church.

So, while we condemn and judge the actions of these designers, and I'm sure their intent was deliberate and the content of their designs was thoughtfully prepared, the entire episode is a mirror of the soul of our society. So, this is how we look, TT.

Soon people might be parading in polo shirts in the hallowed halls of Parliament and lawyers will wear shorts and vests to present their briefs. Bikinis and see-through dresses will be the fashion on the promenades, and at Carnival nudity will be the norm. I hope we can bear that.

So where do we go from here? Apologies made and accepted. The crass will continue to have no class. The revelations of the word will continue to clash with those of the world. The battle lines have been drawn for centuries. There's nothing new under the sun.

So, you win this round, my creative friend, but remember that the longest rope has an end. We will continue to pray and protect our sanctity while others revel in diversity and scanty dress. May God help us all!

PLEASE, NO LIES AS YOU EULOGIZE

NEWSDAY

Friday, 29th November 2019

THE EDITOR:

If some people sat down to think what a eulogy really means, they wouldn't be writing so many lies in the newspapers these days. All those nice things people saying about the man 'who just died', they should be saying the truth instead. If he was a racist, then just say so. He never hid what he did, so why look me in the eye and lie? He was a case of prejudice personified.

So, we want to praise him into eternity with a good eulogy? A eulogy is described as a speech or writing in praise of a person, especially one recently dead. But they lie... eulogies lie. Thou shalt not lie, can be apt at funerals too.

"Say something nice about the man nah, he done dead already," seems to be the mantra for when people leave the earthly scene. It doesn't matter how many wrongs they did in their lifetime; one good eulogy will make it all right. What a fallacy!

We have attended many funerals through the years and saw plenty tears flow for the dearly departed. But we have also seen quite a few sullen faces in the crowd, which masked the anger over the sweet words being said about the dead. When a loved one gets up to give some praise to the memories and legacy of the departed, that's time for niceties not unpleasantries. That is what people call a eulogy.

So, we revel in the glory of the man or woman who just left the scene, even if their life was not so clean. But God be the judge. While we rant and rave, the man going in his grave after saying a prayer to God for salvation in the Christian way, or whatever his belief might be and it's we left to ketch.

After all the praise for the person deceased who sometimes didn't even deserve it, we walk away with a sense of pride. We have done our deed and let all the haters fret. The man must have had at least one good bone in his body, as the old people used to say. So, who am I to judge? The eulogizers can't help but lie about the man today. Go ahead then, just say what you going to say. A hero to many, but he fought for only a few.

So, when we say what we say, till the day that the departed is laid to rest, let's remember that God is the one who gives the final test and the scales of justice will be balanced over yonder, where we will hear the real eulogy read, the one that people cannot see; the one that determines our destiny.

COMMENTARY

PALMISTE... PRESERVE THE HISTORY

NEWSDAY

December 2010

THE EDITOR:

For over ten years, there has been a quiet but concerted effort of appeal to the authorities to consider the establishment of a historical museum site at Palmiste in San Fernando. The area represents the only remaining site of a sugar factory in the south (other than that of Ste Madeleine of course).

In the map of 1889, prepared by Antilles Petroleum Company Limited, the Palmiste estate consisted of several smaller estates including Cedar Grove, Phillipine, Canaan, Bel Air, La Resource and Bachelors Hall. The area still bears the name of some of these sites while others have been lost in the transition.

However, despite the many changes over the years, some relics of the past are still identifiable at various points throughout the community.

Today, one can still see the remnants of a small bridge, which served the trains transporting sugarcane to feed the nearby factory.

It is not uncommon for homeowners in the Palmiste area to find the large ten-foot cistern in their back yards, part of the water collection system of the past. They remain there, too costly to relocate, too precious to destroy.

Letters to the Editor

Miles of rails was cut and used as fence posts for the nearby Palmiste Park. Elsewhere in the area, the chimney of the once proud factory stands, now overgrown with weeds and clingers, but a proud sentinel of the past.

The ongoing quest is to persuade the relevant authorities to support the identification and release of the Palmiste factory as a site worthy of restoration, preservation, and exhibition. The problem has been compounded by the difficulties in securing approvals by the custodians of the property.

Altogether, I have continued to be seriously disappointed in the way we treat our history. As a people, we need to pick up the pride of our heritage, in this case, the celebration of the era when sugar was king and held out its sweet sceptre to our fledging society.

We cannot continue to overlook the significance of emphasizing the importance of our past for the benefit of our children and the future. We have to stop trampling the remnants of our heritage under the guise of progress and indiscriminately destroying or disregarding the voices of our past which speaks volumes to us if we could only listen.

The Palmiste Historical Society is being formed to champion its cause. We join other few but encouraging efforts like the Caribbean Historical Society and the recently formed Petrotrin Historical Society. Our mission is to restore, preserve and exhibit the historical sites at Palmiste.

Indeed, we must appreciate what went before, learn from it, and share the knowledge with children. Our students can visit and visualize the past and gain vital insights into that popular period of our history. They will then be less inclined toward that popular period of our history. They will then be less inclined to appreciate somebody else's history more than their own as they are so readily inclined to do.

With the recent interest in museums and historical sites, one hopes that this appeal would gain sanction and support from the powers that be. The Palmiste Historical Society will certainly be a complement to the beauty of the recently Palmiste National Park, with its heart-shaped pond and landscaped slopes.

This is a call to preserve Palmiste and all other communities. It is a call for us to have a greater sense of pride in our places of interest, not only for ourselves but also for our children and our children's children.
December 2019

KEEPING TIME IN SAN FERNANDO

NEWSDAY

Tuesday, 17th February 2001

THE EDITOR:

The recent installation of a new clock on Chancery Lane in San Fernando is to many a welcome contribution to good timekeeping in the southern city. But to others, it might well be just another architectural addition to the cityscape; or merely a gesture of goodwill.

But like the little boy from my school days story, I stood in my shoes, and I wondered. I pondered on the necessity for yet another timepiece when the times have changed, and people have several other reliable sources for knowing the time. They walk and watch their phones, check their watches, and even hear the radio time-check as they commute.

But there are now four clocks located along the famous Harris Promenade in San Fernando, undoubtedly, to improve the sense of time among the burgesses and visitors to the city. In this way, we can never be out of timing.

The new clock was installed by a group of concerned businessmen, who saw the need to contribute to the improvement of timekeeping in the city. In this case, the clock stands at the western end of Harris Promenade, at the top of Chancery Lane, opposite the San Fernando General Hospital. The project was organised by the outgoing mayor of the city, who almost ran out of time to get the clock installed before the end of his time in office.

So, I even wondered if the clock's location had anything to do with the timekeeping of nurses and doctors and ancillary staff at the institution. The hospital administration must be pleased with such a visible attempt to improve timekeeping options for staff and patients alike. But pedestrians are admonished to take their time while crossing, as the clock stands on the small "island" in the middle of the street.

But I'm still not sure what the four clocks are for. To tell the correct time, to check whether they are synchronous or just to add to the decor. On reflection, the intent is obvious – to help people to be on time, even if they are reminded four times in a short distance. Because as the proverbial saying goes, "anytime is Trinidad time" and four clocks should fix that.

The other three clocks are located on the tower of City Hall, the tower of the Roman Catholic Church (Our Lady of Perpetual Help), and at the corner where High Street meets Harris Promenade at its eastern end.

It's worth noting, that while the St Paul's Anglican Church to the western end of the promenade has no tower clock, it joins the OLPH in providing timely bell chimes, admonishing people to take time to pray to God. That's an important consideration in the short time we have on earth.

But we have all come a long way from watching the shadow cast by the sun, to where we have clocks in high places. There are now more timepieces telling time in our time. Back in the day, the public timepiece was a universal trend, like Big Ben in London. As usual we "follow fashion" and the first clock in San Fernando and the Dial clock in Arima (circa 1898) were installed to give the correct time with morning chimes, as people set about their daily affairs.

Letters to the Editor

But I surmise, that all these clocks on the towers are not for the youths among us. The time for public clocks set in towers has passed. Still, some of us might take a nostalgic glimpse at the old faithful clocks from time to time, and even journey to San Fernando to admire the latest public clock in the country. But I don't expect another clock will be needed any time soon.

When last I checked, all the clocks were carrying the correct time, and the church bells still rang on the hour. The city of San Fernando never had it better in our time.

LET'S FIX THE FLOODING

NEWSDAY
Tuesday, 24 December 2019

THE EDITOR:

There was yet another flood in Barrackpore and the other outlying areas. Residents faced the truth of the geography of the area: they couldn't escape the deluge. It's a very sad situation, but an opportunity for the Government to get something done for the people of such affected areas across the country.

This flooding problem has made heroes of some and fools of many. But we can't continue in this way. We must wise-up and fix this flooding problem. No blame-shifting required. The experience of flooding is real and recurring for those who build houses in areas where flooding occurs. Just a hint of rain and it's flooding again.

But let's not make the same mistake as a former mayor who commented that a calamity falls to those who put themselves in the wrong place. His apparent lack of sympathy cost him his job though he spoke the truth, in a way. But we just cannot continue to build on riverbanks or low valleys and not expect flood.

This situation must also mean something to those living "high and dry" on the hills. We must sympathise and assist families affected by the recent and past floods. They may not have had another option in the past, but we must put a stop to the granting of approvals to construct houses in flood-prone areas.

Letters to the Editor

The rain that is good for the crops, in extreme, is bad for the land. It makes life miserable for those who live in the areas where the rivers flow through yards, across roads and fields on their way to the sea.

It's psychological stress every time the sky turns grey. One official indicated that nothing can be done, in referring to the volume of water that inundated the little villages and left everyone scrambling for higher ground.

So, it's inevitable that the place will flood again and again. As long as the place is flat like that. It's a Bangladesh-type existence in some areas – high tide meets flooded rivers caused by a shower of rain. Living with the ebb and flow. So where do you go? Even if you cut down a hill, it is flooding still. We lament the situation; it's a real conundrum for many among us with climate change being as it is.

It's imperative that we deal with the issue of flooding. We need better mitigation in this situation. There must be improved irrigation and new policies and procedures to address this perennial problem. There must be an allocation of adequate funding and people living on the banks of rivers or on the flood plains must be relocated to higher ground.

The army should set up outposts in strategic areas, with an emergency team tasked to respond in a timely manner. There should be warehouses with relief disaster items located within a short radius of the areas most affected. In addition, we can build levees on the banks of rivers or even create larger catchment areas to contain flood waters.

It might be a herculean task, but it's a vital humanitarian mission for our nation. We need some creativity and the right technology to address this mess. We have to fix our own flooding problem. If we don't do something, we will be praying in vain when the rains come again.

COLUMBUS WAS SEEN IN SANDO

NEWSDAY

14th July 2020

THE EDITOR:

It's time to debunk this Columbus debate. I will not stand by like a statue, while this issue presents a mockery of our heritage and of our native people. We should follow the lead of the people of San Fernando, who dismounted a similar statue from their midst many years ago. For southerners, the ship has already sailed on this matter.

I am convinced that Columbus was seen in Sando. A photo that was taken in 1954 revealed a figure with a striking resemblance standing proudly on Harris Promenade. It was mounted obliquely opposite the old town hall, embellished, with European faces on its facade. It was given the pomp and respect due to the man who 'discovered' the land already occupied by the natives of 'Iere' our beautiful island.

Many persons believe the statue was placed in honour of the famed seafarer. Others contend that it was Lord Harris or some other gentleman of repute, but the real issue is, why was it mounted there in the first place? It begs the question about the present-day contention, which is rife among citizens, as to whether or not the statue in Port of Spain should be allowed to stand.

Some say he is 'pure' history, and he should not be removed. But certainly, we should be able to find someone else from our past to stand in the space. While Columbus was not guilty to some people, others are convinced that his arrival in the region was the channel for the crimes to be committed. He was the man who led the invasion and opened the door for the genocide of the native people.

Although, it was for exploration that he came.... it became exploitation and emasculation without remorse. The aim was to find gold and to save the souls of the native people so that they can give their labour and their talents to the 'deserving' colonizers.

But if a man is found guilty of a crime to humanity, he is removed from society and stripped of all his accolades and credits. So why this guilty man is allowed to freely stand in our company? That statue should be secured in a dim corner of a basement away from the light of day.

Those who fight to retain it are like the 'uncle Toms' of our day, pandering to the massa mentality and perpetuating this fallacy of history. We are aiding and abetting, keeping our children mentally chained to the memories of the atrocities meted out to the hapless natives. There was no consideration for the Indigenous people, the slaves, or the indentured workers who came later. No statue stands in recognition of those who 'benefited' from his famed arrival.

The heart of the matter is that a man is being celebrated as a hero for his bravery to sail the seas, but not considered as the villain that he really was. He must remain a memory in our minds but not a constant reminder of the genocide he caused. Some say that history cannot be erased, but that doesn't mean it has to be forever in our face!

The people of San Fernando never mourned the statue's change of stature. The story of the man should remain in our books and on shelves but not in a public place of adulation for 'discovering 'our nation. We are perpetuating a lie.

But the real mockery of the matter is to see Columbus standing there with a Christian Cross in hand...a symbol of salvation, that was misused to bring abuse, oppression, and exploitation.

Many erroneously align the gory story of Columbus ...discovery, slavery, and genocide...to the glory of the church in its evangelistic fervour. The two ideals were separate and apart. Despite this fact, we must continue to raise the cross in the land, but that Columbus statue should not be allowed to stand!

Sando people wouldn't stand for that!

A SYMBOL FOR SANDO

NEWSDAY

February 8th, 2020

THE EDITOR:

It's as a good time as any to mount a suitable symbol to mark the south entrance to San Fernando. I write this as a student of history and a resident of the second city of our country.

The southern boundary of the city was identified many years ago. It is at the beginning of Mosquito Creek with its unhindered view of the Gulf of Paria. But what is missing is a marker, a sign or especially a monument to speak of our past and as a memorial to those in the future.

The boundary of the city would do well to have an oil pump jack mounted on the small rise to the east side of the entrance to the recently renovated roadway. The pump jack is a fitting symbol indicating the history of oil in the south of the island.

If mounted, it would be just a few miles from Aripero, where the first commercial oil well was drilled back in 1866. Its location will therefore mark the entrance to the rich oil producing fields in the deep south.

The city of San Fernando has seen much growth from the wealth accumulated from the energy sector through drilling and production activities over the years. The nearby refinery grew up from the 1950s and can be seen from the vantage point of the San Fernando Hill. Both are significant landmarks, manmade and natural, for the city.

But the mounting of a symbol – a pump jack – would give significance to the oil history of the city and the area south of the city.

Numerous small drilling efforts dotted the map even within the city limits and nearby communities like Palmiste bear evidence. While beneath our feet runs scores of pipelines, some long forgotten. They traverse the landscape and dot the area with small "Christmas trees" (remnants of oil wells) and the many innocuous signs of gas lines buried along the way.

But even so, the symbol will remind us of the work of the early oil pioneers and serve to represent their efforts and the ongoing nature of oil production in our country.

Fittingly, I believe the inscription could read: "Welcome to the city of San Fernando – A place where pump jacks bow to greet you." Indeed, it reminds us of the hospitality of the people of the southland and the rich legacy of the land, from where "black gold" brought wealth to the coffers of the country and built the city of San Fernando.

A pump jack is what we need to silently speak to passers-by, especially the children and the visitors, as we honour our past and pray that the memory of our oil ventures will forever last.

Meanwhile, an old oil derrick can show the way at the eastern entrance to the city, lighted at night as a beacon. But I think I'm pushing my luck here.

We do need a symbol or a sign that celebrates all that represents south – the oil in the soil, the honourable toil, and the growth of a grateful city. Let the aesthetics and history combine to highlight the truly blessed heritage of our industrial capital.

BETTER ROADS AHEAD IN 2020

NEWSDAY
Friday, 12th January 2020

THE EDITOR:

As we look at the road ahead for the New Year 2020, we envisage all that life has in store for us. But we must first look around at the state of the roads that we have to travel on. Many of the roads that traverse our country are in desperate need of repair. Potholed and patchy, our roads look more like those of a nation in desperation, rather than one with a vision.

So, we step forward in hope that the road ahead will be well paved and maintained, but this has always been a challenge for us. Otherwise, though, we are comforted in the thought that we can continue to dream of the streets of gold that the Bible speaks of.... because our roads here on earth are in such poor and deplorable conditions.

During the recent holiday season, I faced a real challenge getting my overseas visitors to look at the lovely greenery of the countryside, to keep them distracted from the uncomfortable ride along the way. One person eventually asked if all our roads are this bad. 'No,' I answered, 'Just the ones we drive on.'

There's no use in whining about the many mashed-up roads we have to drive on in our country. Wishfully, we need a good solid yellow brick road like in the fairy tale 'Land of Oz.' I have become weary in wondering, why our roadways are in such a poor condition. I'm running out of reasoning. The engineering, the subsurface, the equipment... I am bemused. But then, I see roads built by the US servicemen back in the 1940s that still stand today. Incredible but true.

Then, I wondered more that maybe the bad road conditions are what really slowed down drivers and not only the $1000 fine for speeding. My guess is that people must drive well within the speed limit if they wish to reduce damage to their vehicles. But it all amounts to an uncomfortable driving experience and costly visits to the mechanic.

Recently, while driving behind a speed limit adherent, I saw the driver veer off to the left side of the road and began driving on the shoulder. I realized shortly why he did. The main road was in such a poor state, with several potholes, which were well camouflaged by the saboteur who digs holes in the roads at night to spite the government. 'What a fanciful, ridiculous thought,' I said to myself, and returned my full attention to avoiding the next pothole.

While one would expect a few depressions on the back roads or old cane roads, it is inconceivable why the main roads are pitted, as if they missed out, the last time election paving had come around. 'Pave-the-road 'campaigning seems to be the order of the day; where people drive on smooth roads and forget the rough ride they normally had to contend with. Somewhere along the way, 'Pothole politics' replaced 'Rum and Roti' politics as the main election ploy in our country. That explains it.

But I'm told that the roads are well planned and well paved, but then they only last a few days or weeks maybe. What in the world!? I have had to exclaim.... as I negotiate my way past another pothole. The stress is a real test to the drivers and passengers. Sometimes it feels as how an old stagecoach ride would have been, in the American wild west. Shucks man!

Maybe we need to include 'Pothole Avoidance' and 'How to negotiate around potholes' as part of our learning to drive manual. We can also install the international standard traffic warning sign for uneven roads. And our tourism plans could include an advisory to visitors, to watch out for the potholes and pot hounds, as they visit our beautiful islands. Like our roads gone to the dogs.

Recently, I drove past the pitch lake and realized that the technology that built the roads may have been patterned after the undulating nature of the surface there, with the many small ponds like potholes. No wonder!! Landing in a six-inch-deep pothole on an otherwise smooth main road surface could make a God-fearing man sin his soul. I'm all for a 'Pray as you drive campaign.'

I don't need to make a pitch here for better roads; it's usually on the to-do list of seasonal election campaigns. But it's all a very uncomfortable aspect of driving on our roads; a problem that can be easily resolved with the right approach.

And so, I appeal to the highest authority in the land. Madam President, I am asking for your intervention. We can sing our national anthem even more proudly, as we drive along smooth roadways with our families, friends, and visitors. Save us from this malady, m'lady. These roads will be the death of us. Let's hope and pray for better roads ahead in 2020.

PRAYER IS ESSENTIAL

NEWSDAY

Wednesday, 1ˢᵗ April 2020

THE EDITOR:

Like an x-ray of the soul of the nation, the current pandemic has exposed the reality of many things, one of which is the need for prayer. I commend the Prime Minister and the Minister of Communication for guiding our nation to prayer.

The calling of a National Day of Prayer is not new, but it is essential to deal with the novel virus. So as a people we gathered under the astute leadership of the PM to pray.

We have seen and heard several international leaders publicly call on the name of God for relief from this dreaded disease that is affecting nations across the world. Many have been moved to tears as nations continue to pray.

Meanwhile, the naysayers and doubters have become converts to the truth, realising that there is more to life than the strength and power of oneself. Many manmade measures have come up short in the attempts to bring respite to suffering nations. It's good that we have been wisely preventative in our efforts here in our country.

In the midst of this calamity, there is a rise in the significance of spirituality, as people seek to find God, the Supreme Being who is denied by many among us, including some intellectuals and politicians.

But the cry "Oh God" has become a more common expression as prayers rise to the heavens, as men call on the name of the Lord. Indeed, the strategic resolution of this problem requires both the health workers at the frontline and the spiritual leaders at the "God line."

The Prime Minister even stated in an indirect way that such people think they have a "direct pipeline to God." It's ironic that his words reflected the symbol of the economic wealth and revenue of our nation – the oil pipeline.

The black earth of our countryside is criss-crossed by hundreds of miles of pipelines and gas lines that have given life to the energy sector. Likewise, there has been a spiritual conduit to God that has kept us secure. So much so that people have come to say, "God is a Trini," such is the favour of God that has kept our nation.

As it is important in the oil industry to maintain a flow from the rigs to the pumping stations, to the refinery, so to it is important to ensure that our spiritual channels are clear. Nothing must be allowed to block the flow from God. It is not necessarily the oil in the soil, but our prayers to God that have kept us. As the pandemic creates gloom and oil prices drop low, we know where to go – not to fete and frolic, but to prayer.

When a crisis arises, the cries of the people rise to God to take us out of the mire. As a nation, we have drifted away from the ideals and values that were pillars of our past and the bastions of our future.

And so, this nation turns to prayer as our grandmothers taught us, as our spiritual leaders instruct us. But some of us have found more time to play and less time to pray. We seem to have lost our way, not even able to say, "Oh Lord our God, how great Thou art."

Today, our prayers seem to have been relegated to mere ceremonial utterances and pretences. But now God has spoken, the nations have been shaken and man is on his knees – where he was not inclined to be – to pray. Mr Prime Minister, you have done well. Prayer is essential.

SANDO LIBRARY....
RED AND READY TO BE RESTORED

NEWSDAY

Friday, 10th July 2020

THE EDITOR:

Something needs to be done about that red building in the heart of the city of San Fernando, called the Carnegie Free Library. It is the structure that gives its name to the most popular part of the city. It has become an eyesore and heartache. The building is red and ready for renovation. I am campaigning for its restoration.

The library stands there begging for attention, as our election motorcades drive by year after year. I am calling for urgent and immediate action. The building has become a painful sight to all southerners, near and far. I really cannot comprehend the wisdom that went into its abandonment. It now stands as a sad symbol of our past and our ongoing struggle for standards of excellence.

This beloved edifice has remained unused for years. It has suffered total neglect, due to a lack of due diligence and our unashamed negligence in preserving our historic legacy. There should be a law against this!

We cannot continue to countenance the state of this place. It's a disgrace!! Right in your face!! Certainly, the library is the centre of the city, and we can't miss that! School children pass by every day and wonder what the adults are doing and what we are leaving behind for them.

Why do we let so many things fall apart in T&T? It's something deep in our psyche. We could name many buildings of former glory that shaped our story as a nation, which have been allowed to decay. The San Fernando Library is one such building. To let it waste away is irresponsible, to say the least. But more seriously, it looks like we like it so. It reflects serious decay in our society and a lack of appreciation of our heritage.

Whether, impotence or incompetence, the responsibility for preserving the library has been shirked and shuffled around for years. It has become a shell of itself, seemingly waiting for the demolition hammer. Its splendour tarnished and now imprisoned behind a galvanized fence guarded by a row of thriving vendors.

Enquiring on the restoration of the San Fernando Library has been a real grind. Calls to the relevant authorities revealed a lack of funds, or no plans this year, or that year or any year. The 'powers that be' have failed to acknowledge that the building represents a pride of place and dignity in the southern city.

The San Fernando Public library is the soul of the city. It has helped to raise our standard of literacy and produced many scholars, artisans and articulate men and women for our nation. We need to hear grateful voices rise in support for the edifice which seems condemned to die.

Sando people should rally to this cause and demand that this building be restored to its former glory and change the sad story that is standing at the centre of our southern city. It's the kind of situation that brands us as poor custodians of our heritage!

Even the 100th anniversary of the opening of the Carnegie Free Library passed quietly on March 31st, 2019, without any fanfare or even the sight of a steelband man serenading on a tenor pan.

I cry shame! Shame! Shame! I don't know who is to blame, but the library shouldn't continue to stay in that condition...abandoned, neglected and a poor reflection on the state of our city and our nation. This structure is dear to the hearts of all southerners and deserves our immediate attention. The people of Sando deserve better.

Mr Prime Minister, the San Fernando Library is red and ready to be restored.

COMMENTARY

'POLITICITIS' ALERT!

NEWSDAY

27th July 2020

THE EDITOR:

I have come to accept that there is a real malady in the midst of us.... not the pandemic but the politics... more accurately "politicitis" I hope that my medical friends would indulge me. What has been a pastime or seasonal event, every five years, has morphed into a widespread problem in our society.

The hard-won voting suffrage has become a suffering for many in the nation. No community escapes. And as with any epidemiological problem, it spreads among people who are conditioned to believe that they are immune to infection. But some people are clearly predisposed to strains of the 'politicitis' problem, especially during election time.

I have observed extreme symptoms of radicalism, racialism, and outright bias, leading to crass, irresponsible utterances and irrational behaviour. Social media is 'plagued' with the various symptoms of the condition, as people seem rabidly committed to humiliating themselves and debilitating the nation.

Many years ago, HIV Aids was a scourge and threatened the very life of the community; but the 'politicitis' problem has been evident for years. It's whispered in hushed breath from one person to another. Conversing connoisseurs share it deliberately over a drink or two. And some parents take pains, to pass on the precious family prejudices and traditions, which have now given rise to full-blown vitriolic comments on social media platforms.

Today, young people give vent to their frustrations about having 'contracted' the disease from a parent, co-worker or 'riding partner.' Good history tracing will confirm.

So, we all suffer as the spin doctors work behind the scenes, in an orchestrated effort to colour our political landscape in their favourite hue. Few attempts are made to sanitize the nation from this contagion. There are no weekly briefings, but spasmodic and often irrational statements that defy reason. One calypsonian referred to it as the 'ranting of a mad man,' while others give tolerances for the statements being made in this 'silly season'.

Election time is when 'affected' people walk around with glazed-looking eyes, waving flags, frantically, dancing and prancing with the symptomatic antics of an extreme case of "politicitis." The fever-pitched frenzy of electioneering and campaigning gives rise to outbursts of illogicality and self-destructive utterances. Some of the very symptoms that the good Doctor, Eric Williams, our first Prime Minister tried to prevent.

The divisive diatribe akin to 'politicitis' has been symptomatic of a nation that refuses to take preventive measures, to consider remedial efforts or to try to contain some of the saliva-laden picong on the political platforms. It's wetting after wetting for all political opponents.

The mortality rate and morbidity statistics are high among leaders, but the real intensity remains hidden among the masses. Many men and women have died slow political deaths, having been exposed to the malady as people gather in 'close proximity' in parties and class fraternities.

So, this condition has its own morality, as one well-known politician once said. Even more, ethnic alliances and social connections cause infections that could be traced in our history from colonial times to now.

Many good men turn bad when exposed to this dreaded 'disease.' Only a few live on long to talk about it.

My grave concern is that this thing will be the death of us. Within recent years I have seen strains of the condition manifested even among some religious groups. The rabid ideologists and the fanatical party protagonists have presented themselves brazenly, as acute cases; some of them seem beyond redemption.

And so, we are in a real pika patch, coronavirus in the air, but the social health and history of our nation are plagued by 'politicitis.' Many men have washed their hands from participating in the voting exercise in an attempt to avoid the obvious. But as soon as some people open their mouths to speak, you get evidence of the presence of the condition. Others have refused to even discuss the topic openly for fear of being contaminated.

We are dealing with a condition that we can't seem to avoid. It's corrupting us by every creed and race. We have failed as a nation to diagnose this problem. A lot of us are living in deep denial. This 'politicitis' thing is tearing us apart. It's time to give ourselves a good check-up before it takes us down as a nation.

The prognosis is not good for the democracy of a fledging nation like ours. But the vaccine is available. We must teach the children to love, not hate. We have to increase our tolerance and respect each other's space and views, whether we win or lose. We have to tone down the rhetoric of hate and stop the lies. These things will cause our democracy to die.

Thank God that COVID 19 didn't get us, but let's be careful how we let 'politicitis' infect us. A good dose of love taken three times a day and distancing ourselves from talk of race and hate will keep this dreaded disease at bay.

LETTERS TO THE EDITOR

MAKE NATIONAL DAY OF PRAYER PERMANENT

NEWSDAY

Tuesday, 22 June 2021

THE EDITOR:

The Christian Council of San Fernando calls for a National Day of Prayer and thanksgiving to be permanently included on the TT calendar.

As human beings, we tend to credit improvements and successes to the mechanisation of men and the wisdom of our ways, because by nature we are inclined to exclude God in our praise. But no chapter of our lives is written without prayers and divine intervention in our affairs.

We rest assured in our faith that when a nation calls for his grace and blessings God responds. We encourage all leaders to include prayer in their regime for good health and success.

For many, the practice of prayer is usually left as a knee-jerk response and incidental to the processes of life. We should take note of this observation and seek to maintain a relationship with the divine through our portals of prayer.

Over the years, we have assigned days for many celebrations and commemorations, but not for prayer and thanksgiving. Now is the time to declare a National Day of Prayer and thanksgiving which will give us an opportunity to publicly acknowledge God in our dealings.

Other nations have set aside a day of prayer on their calendar, including the US, with an official day celebrated on the first Thursday in May of each year since 1952.

We trust that this submission meets with the approval of those entrusted with the responsibility to lead our nation. We suggest that the first Thursday of July each year be designated as the National Day of Prayer and thanksgiving.

We will continue to pray for our nation, the region, and the world as we look forward to the celebration of a National Day of Reverence, such as is consistent with any God-fearing country.

APOSTLE TERRENCE HONORE
on behalf of the ministers
Christian Council of San Fernando

MORE BACCHANAL WITH CANCELLING OF CARNIVAL

NEWSDAY

Tuesday, 13th October 2020

THE EDITOR:

The cancellation of Carnival has been met with great consternation by certain people in our nation. The prospect of the national Carnival being cancelled is unthinkable to some people. Well, maybe someone should think it over and put the decision in reverse. But I fear that the Prime Minister wouldn't "back back" on this one.

It's clear that many have embraced Carnival as our life and others, their very livelihood. From the early days of Canboulay to the present time of jam and wine, this season of the year has become part of the lifeblood of the nation. Some people even think that you "cyah cancel Carnival, that is we culture!"

In the past, not even rain could stop the Carnival. But these days, the situation has changed, the covid19 virus is king over Carnival. All protesting people have to bow to this monarch of worldwide fame or face the grave consequences. So maybe, yes, it's time to quarantine Carnival.

But the fight to keep the Carnival has been strong since massa days when the colonial elite frowned on the festivity. It would seem that the powers that be, have always sought to curtail the freedoms of the people to express themselves, to "dingolay" as they say.

Some may even think the decision is capricious and uncaring. But the announcement of the cancellation has caused the authorities to once more lock horns with the masqueraders, the panmen and the partygoers. "Somebody will have to pay the devil for this one," I could hear the old masmen say.

So, can we really cancel Carnival? It's "in we blood," in the houses and in the street. We are bound to fete, it seems. Some people just live to love the bacchanal. Nothing can replace the chance to "mash-up de place," with decibels that raise hell for quiet residents and rhythms that reveal the anatomy of our women who seem inclined to be dressed in less and less. Carnival has its people.

Yet, some of us might have a concern, as we witness the extremities of the festivities, but the cancellation is another matter. The nation will be in a state if there's no time for Carnival – that's from October to March of the following year. From preparation to gyration, it's the life of the nation. Covid19 "could kill some people dead," but they rather their Carnival instead. No rationale could replace the bacchanal. So they say.

To stop the Carnival will bring out the "wajank" in people. But the cancellation is all about trying to save people from one malady at the expense of another.

Carnival is not "all ah we." But some of us beg to differ.

Some think Carnival is an expression of art and creativity, but many contend it has become sheer vulgarity, as the debate goes on. But in the midst of the argument, the PM's announcement of the cancellation of the national Carnival is causing more bacchanal.

Some would agree that the postponement of the festivity would benefit both the physical and spiritual health of the nation. But it's not only for covid19 restrictions. We need a time-out to consider our ways and "give

God praise children," as the calypsonian sang. Not in the prancing and dancing but in the repenting and confessing.

So, the PM wants to put Carnival in confinement from the virus. That might not be a bad idea after all. But then again, we could just extend the period of Lent for a year. I'm just saying.

COMMENTARY

LET'S KEEP SUNDAY SACRED

NEWSDAY

Saturday, 27 February 2021

SUNDAY IS the soul of the nation. It is more than just a fanatical religious preoccupation. There is a reason why the day was woven into the fabric of our society. We have to save Sunday.

Historically, the practice of reserving a day for rest was the best thing for a fledging nation. It was biblical in intent and economical in its effect. It offered intangible rewards such as resting from the labours of life and connecting with the divine.

Most of that has changed, somewhat. Like the ebbing tide that erodes our shoreline, the will and ways of men have shaped this part of our existence and changed our perspective on the day. But there are grave consequences for the nation that does not seek their God and prefers to make Sunday like every other day.

It is so sad what has happened to Sunday, once a day of worship. Our fathers failed to instil in us the respect for the divine and the restful time that the day offers. For many, it's only time to play and dingolay, or even to make some more money. While a few faithful find respite in the solemn assembly of prayer, their hands are raised in praise and sometimes in protest at what our Sunday has become.

We have failed as a people to extol the virtues of the day. Although it's justifiable that we should engage our time and energy towards acquiring wealth, the essence of our lives cannot be trifled away by sacrificing the only day we have for rest. Sunday must be set aside for the purpose of praise and thanksgiving and relaxation.

We must remember the fate of the great city of Rome and the debauchery, the wantonness, the festivities, and flagrant disorders of the day. The same demise is certain for our nation if we reject the formula for success that is found in the wisdom of a day of rest.

It's interesting that the recent virus has caused us to rethink our position, making almost every day like a Sunday. We now have plenty of time to rest and reflect. Of consequence, we now give ourselves to quiet deliberation of life and its challenges. That was God's plan from the beginning.

In past times, the law protected Sunday, limiting labour and the opening of bars and businesses, but we have since "flipped" on the importance of the day. The old ordinances have been left in the dusty corners of the library of laws. The common law as an astute reflection of the soul and intent of men in their normal duties has revealed where we are as a nation. Is it then not prudent, just, and fair that we should preserve the sanctity of the day called Sunday?

To violate the sacredness of Sunday is to pronounce judgment on ourselves as a nation. The day that was essential to our family life, a day that would cause men to pause and reflect and recharge their "batteries" for another go at life, that day is dying and so is the soul of the nation.

Though some people have kept the faith, they are few and fewer each day. The churches are emptier, the beaches are fuller, and the rum shops are ranking. Meanwhile, the many devious ways of man are changing God's plan from a time to rest to a time of leisure and pleasure and doing dastardly deeds.

There is a price to pay for surrendering Sunday to the frivolities of life. We may think that we contribute more to the economy by reducing the importance of Sunday, when in fact we are in denial and do our children and ourselves a grave injustice with this diabolical ploy.

We have sauntered our way into contemporary time, moved by the subtle seductions of popular culture, trends and wayward ideologies. The Sunday morning time for worship has been nullified by the need to rest or hit a beach or two and what has evolved is a callous deviation from the norm.

The exigencies of our time seem to be winning the argument for us to continue to change the day from the way it was designed. But all change is not progress and there is a consequence for our actions if we continue to misuse and abuse Sunday in the way it has been done.

So, to those among us who care to retain the respectfulness of the day, to make time for family and friends, to reflect, to recharge and find a place to worship and pray, I commend you. Let us be the remnant that holds this day to be sacrosanct to our society. We are the silent heroes who must take a stand against the marauding minds and missions of the greedy and the heady-minded – those lovers of pleasure rather than lovers of God.

Let us keep the sacredness of Sunday in its rightful place, as central to the resolution of problems in our nation. We have to preserve the order of things, or the disorder will destroy us. Let's save Sunday for our nation's sake!

COMMENTARY

DEFEATING OUR POST-COVID19 DEMONS

NEWSDAY

Thursday, 28th May 2020

THE EDITOR:

THE TRUE character of a person is seen in times of crisis. Likewise, the real nature of a nation is revealed in calamitous times. We are a people who care and even share, but there is a dark side to our demeanour. We gossip like our life depends on it and litter a lot in thoughts, words, and deeds.

This present virus crisis has laid bare the underbelly of the monster in our midst – our self-defeating, self-destructive propensity that became more evident with each day of the covid19 crisis.

Topical it is, in our tropical paradise, where people live in denial, nonchalant, with a don't-care-damn look on their faces. Who needs masks? There seems to be no reason to get serious about what is about us. The storm will pass as it did before. We know this all too well. There seems to be a nihilistic approach to life that confuses me.

Simply put, it's a perplexing thought. We can't seem to change our clothes when they get dirty by the stains of racialism and nepotism and all the other isms that we encounter. Our suicide rate is low, but we are killing ourselves softly, as we go from day to day and taking our children in tow.

Unlike the fabled man with the Midas touch, whatever it seems we lay our hands on diminishes in value due to the demons that beset us. The monsters in the closet come out to play on Carnival Day – that's all year through.

We continue to play the fool with our destiny. Our gratitude to God is diminishing as we dingolay with greed and false prosperity. Our hands are soiled with oil and our fields of green remain uncultivated, as we saunter along in time.

This pandemic reveals a people not quite ready for change, contending with each other for scraps of popularity across the political divide. We seem to prefer to see each other die, unaware that when that happens, we die too. There is no disguise to the demise that is upon us. The music has played, and the charade continues, we seem oblivious to the precipice that we face as a nation. Dancing and cavorting to our deaths.

Economics be damned! It's about how much we can get for ourselves, how much we can feed the greed within our souls, the callous nature of the monsters we entertain in our thoughts and who sit at our tables and spout vitriolic stuff on the social media.

The crisis among us reveals the torment inside us. We have scared our souls with the searing passions that drive us to despair, even when we deny it and shout back loudly over the voice of reason in our ears.

It's real tears I tell you. Maybe not so much for us as for the children, even unto the third and fourth generation, as the Bible says. The sins of the fathers and indeed the mothers and all the others still sully our flag that flies tattered in the wind. In a mind's-eye view, you see the torn fringes and tottering pole of our destiny.

Proud we are to be true Trini, but the truth of who we really are is distorted in the mirror that speaks to us each day. We deny the distorted faces and practise our "colonial graces" as we dance across the grand stage of life.

We kindle strive to survive. We love little and stir up the pot of racial prejudice and give vent to our frustrations for a day or two with each issue. When will we ever learn that what we do to each other comes back to haunt us? So, while we flaunt our ill-gotten wealth, we sicken the health of the nation. Change or die is the banner before us.

This covid19 crisis makes me cry, not just for the sick or dying, but for a nation that needs to see that we are imploding but not knowing – our prejudice is showing, our undergarments are revealed to the world.

It is clear in this crisis that we need to practise the one-love we preach. The priest and parishioners speak and sing but in real life, it's a different thing.

We have done well as a nation but it's not over as yet. The corruption, domestic abuse and other concerns are still there. We must let our divine connection guide us and help us to be all that we ought to be.

The virus is around us, but let's contend with the crisis within us and pray that we defeat the demons of our nation's destiny.

LETTERS TO THE EDITOR

LEAD ON, MINISTER COX

NEWSDAY

Tuesday, 29th June 2021

THE EDITOR:

The letter titled "Clear sign of poor, failed leadership" in the June 16 Newsday seemed to vilify the hardworking Minister of Social Development and Family Services, Donna Cox. The letter was well-intentioned, but its content was somewhat misleading regarding the matter of performance and leadership of the minister. So, I beg to differ.

I take no offence to the author's right to write, but it was clearly a wrong representation of the performance of the minister. We must not attempt to ascribe dishonour to whom honour is due and the ongoing efforts by the minister and her team are credible by any standard.

As the flagship of the Government in caring for the less fortunate among us, the efforts of that ministry have been commendable. So, I lament this sad and misaligned attempt to malign the work of the ministry, which has been one of the hardest hit ministries with the onset of the covid19 pandemic.

It has set about the task of rebuilding from the past and setting new horizons for the ministry to meet the needs of vulnerable people in our society. Cox has reflected the Government's good intention to right the wrongs and provide relief for those who need it most.

The recent special subvention from the Ministry of Finance provides an excellent base to implement the much-needed improvements to the ministry's operations and give the hard-working staff a chance to get further ahead of things. The release of funds is a good sign that the leadership of the Government is supportive of the efforts of Cox and her team. I accept this as a fact.

But then why would someone ascribe blame to a fledgling ministry that only last month launched a new effort to improve the online distribution of funds to the population? The special initiative called the Income Support Grant is intended to accelerate the process to get much-needed assistance to the needy. The effort will reduce the need for people to stand in long lines waiting on their stipends, grants, or allowances. I look forward to improvements in the service offered.

Cox's effort is a bright light in the midst of the gloom of our present situation. I look with hope to the time when all support measures are fully implemented and digitised. The ministry is clearly set to achieve the high standards it has set for itself to lift the disadvantaged among us to a more comfortable and rewarding life.

I look to the leadership of people like Cox to address the ills of society and help to close the gap on the provision of care to the less fortunate among us. I continue to have hope, especially during this covid19 pandemic that the needs of the vulnerable would be adequately addressed.

As for the detractors, their energies might be better suited to planting a backyard garden or supporting a worthy cause as we help to build our country, rather than casting aspersions on the improving processes of our social system. So, whether this attack is on the person or the political party, it is in poor taste, especially when referring to proven leadership.

The ministry cannot be judged on what a few people say, but rather on the delivery of services to the oppressed, poor, and needy. Madame Minister, lead on!

APOSTLE TERRENCE HONORÉ
San Fernando

STOP THE 'ACTING' FOR TOP COP

NEWSDAY

Wednesday, 22nd December 2021

THE EDITOR:

It must be the crime of the century in Trinidad and Tobago that we continue to keep appointing an Acting Commissioner to head the police service.

While I am elated and grateful to God that the position was finally approved, I realize that it must mean little to the criminal element, who are comfortable in the chaos caused by the ongoing saga of the poor handling of crime from a governance level.

It's not the fault of the police in the ranks that they can't seem to produce a leader appointed and approved by the authorities to keep law and order in the land. The selection of a leader is not their responsibility; it's the authorities that be who seem to keep getting it wrong.

We must remember that crime is the number one problem that we have to contend with in this little republic, but we just can't seem to get it right. That is a crime in itself. There must be a law to correct that.

But who is keeping score of the long list of fails and the litany of woes of the police service, since they were promoted from the days of wearing short pants? Who is charged with the responsibility to address these ills?

Letters to the Editor

The crime problem is essentially one of leadership; it seems that many people have tried to make it political. The lack of an appointment is a disappointment to the law-abiding people of our country. Now the opposition chose to abstain again.

What is the matter with our leaders that they can't get this simple task right? From the ongoing 'soap opera' of the Police Services Commission to the interference by those with axes to grind; while God-fearing people look on in dismay and old grannies continue to pray.

I am told the last 'colonially' appointed white commissioner was James Porter Reid M.G.M. QP (1966-1970). He was followed by the first black CoP, Mr. Francis Eustace Bernard M.G.M QP. (1970-1973). Then there was the local white appointee, Mr. Claud Anthony May (1973-1973). They were all duly appointed to their positions by the powers that be.

But it didn't matter the colour of the commissioner it's how we handle the white collar, pink colour, green collar or red collar set of 'rainbow' crime we have in our country.

As it appears, the curtain closed on the colonial era and the 'acting' continued to this day. Someone in their wisdom thought it best to have the top cop in an acting capacity, even until the end of their time in the service when they walked away with a lesser pension.

It is obvious that the well-intentioned 'career officers' who have performed their duties to protect and to serve have found themselves coming short of the high standards set by the academically inclined commission when it came to promotion to the CoP position.

But here we go with an acting commissioner again. We are watching too many movies. Arguably, few governments if any, in any country, have had so many 'actors' to lead their police force. It must be another record of which we can't be proud. Somebody has to start getting this right so that law-abiding people can sleep well at night.

It's an indictment to this day that the police service is in such a state, in our beautiful Republic. There seems to be little respect for the men and women who conscientiously work to serve and protect. We are operating in this institution like a back street parlour unable to recruit and retain a commissioner, time after time. But the real problem is not with the police, but with those who hold the reins, appearing to treat us all like animals of burden to carry the load of their incompetence. They are presenting convoluted clauses that cause us so much grief and cause crooked cops and ghetto gangsters to rejoice.

We even tried the good ole Scotland Yard and our 'migrated' family friends in Canada sent us a 'Mountie', but things got sadder than it has been, since the days when Commissioner Randolph Burroughs reigned, raided, and put criminals to flight.

What is it that keeps us from functioning in good governance, with respect to the appointment of the top position, to handle the biggest problem that we have faced as a young nation? This is yet another acting position to lead the fight against the avalanche of crime. What a disgrace!

Crime is like a runaway horse and the jockey is given permission to put one foot in the stirrup. The parliament and the opposition and the commission seem to be in collusion to keep us in confusion. The situation makes us all fools to the wise and a reason for the badjohns among us to party.

So, there must be a natural progression from a deputy commissioner to the top position. Let's remove the 'acting' title that has become the 'default position' for naming of a CoP. It reflects a lack of due diligence by the authorities towards the hard-working police officers and the people of Trinidad and Tobago.

We must stop the 'acting' and having people directing the task of crime fighting from the sidelines and hindering the police in doing their duty. What is evident is that the top cop remains without the authority to act to the full extent of the law.

But things got worse the other day, when the 'newly minted' Acting Commissioner McDonald Jacob was quoted as saying, in a newspaper report, 'that since mid-October there was no sitting CoP for the first time in the history of the service.' That is backwardness!

I believe the authorities should continue acting in the best interest of the country, but the Commissioner of Police must stop acting and be confirmed in the top position as an act of good faith and commitment to fighting crime. Let's appoint the man to the position. No more acting please

PROMISES SPOKEN, PROMISES BROKEN.

NEWSDAY

Monday, 14 February 2022

THE EDITOR:

AN ELECTION promise not kept is a stain on any political party and pain for people of any community. This has been a central part of our political history. In fact, the performance of a government might well be measured by how many promises are fulfilled rather than what was promised on the political platforms.

In the old days, a man was as good as his word. That was an excellent measuring stick for any performance. Likewise, in the field of politics, where tricks of the trade sometimes outweigh the trade, we have to be careful to consider integrity in public office, including where have all the promises gone.

The balancing of the scales should fit into our schema, where the goodies offered by the political parties are placed on one side and the practicable things on the other side. To quote the good book, Daniel 5:27: "Thou art weighed in the balances, and art found wanting."

The glowing promises of the platform speeches, the flowery "slanguage" of articulate artisans of the art of politics fill our minds with admiration and move our hands to stain our fingers, to vote for worth, not worthless promises. It's plenty icing, but little cake – sweet, but most times lacking in substance.

Political parties should be made to pay for promises not kept. There should be a demerit system assigned to each party on the road after the election. Plenty of promises mean you have more to account for and a less gullible people would revise the strategy that got them voting and hoping for changes. We need some political promises police.

It always seems to be a case of spoken promises, broken promises.

Like a bride to the proverbial altar, voters are led to believe in the sweet lyrics and vows made, but alas, we have to live each five-year term with a set of unfulfilled promises. After the election, we wake up to find that many of the vows spoken have been callously broken.

Political parties driving up the road in their motorcades will say and sing anything to get voters to put on the "political ring," then its horn all the way down the road. Fancy flags and paraphernalia flying high, but after the election, most of the promises are gone with the wind. Some politicians wouldn't give a tart or a glass of mauby for your voting effort.

Even the famed bards of Barbados, The Merrymen, once sang, "Ring ting ting...every year is the same thing, all you do is promising...well you promised me a house and a motorcar." It seems like every election is the same thing, all they do is promise. Many voters become haters because they are denied some of the rewards from the success of the election victory, not realising that all the euphoria might only be for some of the party faithful and not for them.

After the election, finger stains only last for a day or two. But ink remains longer than some promises uttered on the political platforms. As soon as some campaign promises are spoken, they die a sudden political death. Politicians say whatever they want and hope the voting public forgets. But our memory is longer than twine. So, rum and roti and a little gyration by an inebriated supporter can't take away the stain and the shame of broken political promises.

Something seems to go wrong between when the promise is said and when the promise is dead. We have to do some forensics to determine what is killing the promises. Many politicians put their heart into it, but two ticks in time and promises are done. They need to exercise prudence and good sense, to avoid the pretence that passes for promises. We don't need outside observers to see that broken promises are killing us. There is a case for political abuse of the population.

The book of wisdom Ecclesiastes says, "It is better to promise nothing than to promise something and not be able to fulfil it." Remember that when we promise, we promise to God and not just to man. So, let's promise on, but promise well. Unkept promises are like living in hell on Earth.

Meanwhile, the list of broken political promises is extensive, one political party adding to another while the people continue to suffer. The architects of our demise write in glossy manifestos but fail to implement the full measure of the intent of the party promises. I have been around long enough to see what failed promises have done to us as a people. There needs to be some real soul-searching when we promise with one hand and take away with the other.

But we must praise God for the promises kept – as few as they might be. A highway extended, some houses built, but the nation is still on stilts, propped up by promises that haven't been kept for years. It seems that glorious, glowing words are not easily kept in this paradise of ours. But where there is a crime there is a cause. To fix it we must declare only what can be truthfully done. After the election is won, under God's good sun, please let all the good promises spoken remain unbroken.

SHUFFLING THE POLITICAL DECK

NEWSDAY

Wednesday, 23rd March 2022

THE EDITOR:

These are times when our card-playing days reflect on our political ways. This came to mind when I heard of the recent announcement by the government to change the portfolios of some ministers. It's much like the act of shuffling the deck of cards. Or so I thought.

But while it matters little to many, some among us take great stock in analysing the significance of such a move made by those in power. While we ponder the politicians' posture, like poker players sitting across the table of life, staring down each other and wondering at the real meanings behind the shift and shuffle? But in the craft of politics like the game of cards, shuffling, although sometimes necessary, can make things either worse or better for the protagonists.

In a search for clarity on the subject, I sought the Cambridge dictionary which defined the word shuffle verb (MOVE AROUND) ' to move similar things from one position or place to another, often to give an appearance of activity when nothing useful is being done' But I expect that there would be differing views on this interpretation, in our context, given our different political persuasions.

But to the layman, shuffling is a simple task of moving the cards from side to side. But there are cards that you shouldn't put too close to others, and some just wouldn't fall in line. Every leader must have an 'ace in the hole', I am told. But sometimes it seems that you cannot hide the jack far enough, no matter how well you move around the cards. At other times it seems like you just have to throw them all into the air and see where they fall.

But seriously, there must have been much study for this dramatic move. Like the SEA students getting set for their examinations, the leadership must have stayed up many nights studying the cards to get it right. But the questions still hang in the air. Who to put next to whom? Should I shuffle this way or the other? But like in the game of All Fours, care must be taken with the action, as the opposition is quite adept at 'hanging the jack'.

Shuffling moves seem more like chess than a game of cards. Political parties, opinion leaders and strategists studying the subtle movements of others... looking into the eyes of those on the other side of the seating in parliament, shouting and throwing picong, with all the antics, to disturb and distract, to get each other to make wrong moves instead of prudent governance.

But those are the things that keep you up late at night when you hold the reins of government. You are tempted to do the shuffle and say like our first Prime Minister 'Let no donkey bray!' And you can't let the swearing or the plaintive cries of the resigning players make you take your eyes off what is on the table. It's only a small economic pot we've got.

But shuffle as you may, or shuffle as you might, there is a science to this practice, to know how this thing is done...it is as important as knowing how to play the game. Like the late Kenny Rogers said in his country and western classic song "You've got to know when to hold them, know when to fold them.... and if you're gonna play the game boy, you gotta learn to play it right..."

So, every five years the people will call for a change of players and the game begins again. Then eager-eyed senators will deck off in their Sunday best and sit in the Senate among the crafty who know how to play themselves well...that's how the game is lost or won. But sometimes as the drama unfolds, one lowly minister might just begin to think he's a king, or another might give in to a corruption thing...or one might just get too tired of the bacchanal. Such are the dynamics of the political deck of cards. The leader has to avoid a headache, thinking hard about the next move to make. Because the truth is, you could shuffle the cards to the side but incompetence you can't hide.

Ultimately, the political 'game of cards' is won, not just by the way you choose to play but by how well you learn to shuffle. When you shuffle the deck, you have to be careful as some cards fall away or just disappear, fading from the front bench into political oblivion. But even the best card player knows that you must be keen and sharp before and after you decide to shuffle the deck.

Sometimes, the leader keeps the pack in their back pocket, waiting for the change of players at the table at the next sitting of the senate, as the right time to show the 'hand'. There must be wise timing in the shuffling. When you have the right suite it's sweet, but sometimes things could get bitter before they get better. There are times when you know you just have to shuffle the deck and say... What the heck!!

But then again, I am not an expert on political shuffling, but I must say just remember to always pray before you make your play!

TIME TO CLEAN OUT THE WAR BUNKERS!!

NEWSDAY

Monday, 4th April 2022

THE EDITOR:

I have recently resorted to a prayer here and there regarding the Ukraine /Russian conflict. After all, it seems so far removed from our idyllic shores.... our paradise seems still secure and protected. But we have had to think again, not just about the sad atrocities one would expect as a consequence of war, but just how far the sparks of war can fly.

As a post-colonized people, we have shifted from the quasi-freedom of independence to republicanism and jumped into the big pond to fend for ourselves in a world full of wars. So, there must be alertness to the fact that the conflict can affect us economically or even strategically in the 'minefields' of the geo-political world.

As wars and rumours of wars continue to be an ever-present threat to our stability and comfort, we must not be indifferent to the realities of mounting conflicts, latent, perceived, or real, across the globe. Our alertness must be reflected in the way we handle the upkeep of our military system, and how we 'man our defences'.

So, we must go back to the drawing board and review where we are as a nation in terms of military readiness. Are we prepared to protect our patch of paradise? Like a Pompek barking at a Pitbull, it seems a miss-match against the mighty nations, but we must still resort to 'showing our teeth' to hold on to the cherished space we call our own.

Now is a good time to consider the state of our national defences. The recent and ongoing Ukraine /Russian conflict has brought the issue of national security full and centre to our considerations.

Since the days after World War II, we have maintained our residential regiment in the 'hole' in Chaguaramas. The battalion deserves a whole lot more than what they have been given and that includes the need for an updated, modernized military system.

The once intact US military base of operations was partly built by 'Trini hands' under the guidance of the US engineers. Back then, working on the base provided much-needed income for skilled and unskilled workers from Trinidad and a few of the other Caribbean islands. It was also a sweet treasure trove for the 'Jean and Dinah ladies' immortalized in the famous calypso sung by the Mighty Sparrow. But they would all be shocked to know that we let so much of their efforts go to ruins. We seem to be feting while our defences decline.

I am not warmongering or anticipating conflict, but it is the undeniable responsibility of every country to maintain a standing army or defence force, as in our case. But the need to address the system of military defence of the island continues to miss the headlines and seems absent from the minds and the manifestos of our political parties.

'Let the jungle take it over' seems to have been the position taken by many, while the corruption-laden gains continued to shift hands over the years. Our annual budget for military funding misses the need to modernize our national defence system. We have been putting second-hand resources where first-world infrastructure and systems are needed.

Meanwhile, our men and women, dress up in smart uniforms, parading once or twice a year to the strains of music. The sounds of the national anthem fading into the nearby hills, as we stand to rue the fact that we have not maintained or improved what was inherited from the United

States forces. We have to go beyond the pomp and ceremony of our celebrations, to recognize the historic significance and the military importance of the abandoned bases of World War II.

I say it's fitting time to 'bring back' the bases at Wallerfield or Carlson Field and the various installations at La Brea, Pointe-a-Pierre and elsewhere. We must review the once well-laid network of military operations, even to protect ourselves from ourselves, and the don't-care-damn attitude that has left most of the system in ruins.

In the words of the much-loved song by Marjorie Padmore, 'We must take pride in our liberty.' We may not have fought for our freedom by military action, but we must do our best to preserve and improve what we've got... by any means necessary.

Let's clean out the bunkers, make them tourist destinations if we must, or even just a history project for a university class, but we are compelled to continue restoring and upgrading our military system to the highest standard for the safety and security of our beautiful nation.

COMMENTARY

FAITH IN FARMING

NEWSDAY

Friday, 24 June 2022

RECENTLY, a government minister raised the talk of establishing a farm school for youths in the Moruga area. The announcement was treated to the usual ten-day talk shop in the media. The commentators talked and counter-talked, but it all melted down like bhaji in a hot pot on a sunny day.

It was for the "umpteenth" time that the agriculture conversation briefly took centre stage. It sounded like a good idea when it was aired. So, I ask, what became of the farm school talk?

The fact that we are once again getting serious about farming has brought us to this place of good talk, or was it just ole talk? It is an opportunity to get some down-to-earth solutions to our economic problems.

Over the years the leaders of our nation's economy have been more content to raise tank farms than food farms. We were more satisfied to take the oil out of the soil than to put seeds in the ground. We continue to reap bitter rewards…paying a high price for our folly.

Back in the day, the preferred lease farming of our oil-producing fields gave good yields to our economy, but now our lands are stained with oil, dotted by "Christmas trees" (capped oil wells) instead of fruit trees on the dozens of abandoned estates across the country.

In the 1950s, the great debate for economic development held sway and learned men like Sir Arthur Lewis and others debated industrialisation by invitation or by indigenous agricultural development.

But as far back as 1932, Sir Norman Lamont of the Naparima Agricultural Society in San Fernando had argued for farm schools to be built along with the industrial schools. But instead, the technical schools were favoured to grow the energy sector and agriculture has been suffering ever since.

Today, we stand with little oil in hand, still mocking and shaking our heads at the land. Too hard to till, we 'fraid the soil. Farming is hated even by the incarcerated. Working the land remains a painful thought to many who carry the memory of slavery in their blood, but less so for those who were indentured to serve. But it all adds up to a woeful neglect of the wealth beneath our feet.

There is a hindering spirit that pervades the land. The continued demise of the agricultural enterprise is no surprise. It may be a hangover from colonial days when sabotage and withholding labour were the only resistance against the oppression of the slave masters.

Today, we command our own destiny, but we're still trying to rescue the tank farms instead of the food farms to sustain the economy. We seem to have lost our faith in farming.

We are seriously harming our economy by not farming the land. The sight of thousands of acres of uncultivated land has been painful to the eyes and unkind to our pockets. Our governments have followed each other in cue, seemingly without a clue about how to solve the plethora of problems caused by a lack of farming the land.

The attempts to address the seriousness of this economic dilemma are reflected in White Papers, grandiose mega farm schemes and other foreign models ill-suited for our development.

So, we must see the Moruga farm school announcement as a well-intentioned attempt to give agriculture a chance. Let us dream then that once again we will dance the cocoa in the hills and sing the songs of economic freedom. That's good food for thought.

I am told the land in such places as the Naparimas (San Fernando area) was fertile and yielded much produce to the early planters. But we have raised houses instead. People are grabbing the arable land for streets and concrete and glass monstrosities. I borrow from the Bible when I quote, "We are ever learning and never coming to the knowledge of the truth" (Bible 2Tim 3:7-8).

Our affluence has courted the influence of foreign tastes. We killed the sugar cane and the cocoa, the coconuts, and the limes; nothing it seems is good enough for us to grow. At least not in enough quantities to put food on our dinner tables, or to reduce any of our $5 billion food import bill.

All the "buy local" and "support local farmers" campaigns have withered in the wind. The currency of oil and gas has created a dependency on foreign lifestyles. Like a woman in pregnancy, we have craved for what we hardly need, like appetites for the apple and grapes and the insatiable tastes for other things from foreign lands.

The fruits of our labour may never stand against the produce from the metropolitan countries. Just as it was with beet sugar in the sugar cane days. But we must continue to have faith in farming and planting the land, if not only for local consumption.

Some locals even travel to work as seasonal workers on crops "in the cold" and then see the product packaged and shipped back to our land for consumption, without consideration for what can be grown in our own backyard. It is hard to digest...the fact that agriculture remains the "neglected child" of our economic development.

May God help us to put right where we have gone wrong. We need to use the community centres and other available facilities to teach the next generation to secure the future of our food. We must face the stark realities of a lopsided economy that excite analysis among the economists but give little reprieve to the pragmatists among us.

So, the idea of farm schools should have its day in the sun. The heady times of crazy oil drilling, of exploration and exploitation by the men in white shirts and khaki pants are long gone. We were well schooled in the tastes for what our colonial bosses possessed, now its crucial time to "stir up our faith" in a total local flavour.

In our efforts to bring balance to the economy, we must implement more tangible efforts to support local farming. What we need is the right mix of subsidies and incentives that will stimulate growth in the industry. This can be bolstered by a network of secondary-level farm schools across the country.

So, above all the "jhanjhat" and political promises, let us put our money where our mouth is – to fix our food problem, cultivate a new mindset and restore our faith in farming the land.

COMMENTARY

TIME TO TEST THE TALK

NEWSDAY

Wednesday, 7th July 2020

AS TRINIS, we love a good ole talk, but some people continue to push the limits of fair speech with the type of words being uttered in Parliament and in public. The recent, much-talked-about exchanges between two leading politicians have drawn comments from all sides. Given all that has transpired, I think it's time for us to test the talk that reaches our ears and steers our hearts.

Some speakers show good sense in their utterances, but there are others who continue to fill the airways with "out-of-timing" words and phrases. Bad words can have dangerous consequences.

The seriousness of what we say does not only relate to what is recorded in the Hansard in Parliament, or the copious notes taken in the public courts, but to all the talk we talk. We will all have to be judged one day for all we say.

As Jesus Christ said, "…everyone will have to give account on the Day of Judgment for every empty word they have spoken (Matt. 12:36 NIV). It's a tough thought, but till then we must responsibly test everything we say, privately and in the public domain.

We must practise word usage but avoid abusage. We are told that English is a hard language to learn and even harder to understand. Sometimes the idioms get in the way, but often it's the idiots who make it difficult to comprehend. Some people "populate" social media with hyped talk, the kind that flows freely, like flatulence after a chataigne feast.

Now, with the inflation and unbearable increases in food and other consumables, it's reassuring to think that talk remains cheap. But we must be mindful that the courts of law have frequently ordered people to pay high prices for defamatory remarks. Sometimes the law seems to rule in favour of people offended by some "true true fatigue," but generally the legal system compensates victims of vicious talk.

There seems to be too much character assassination in the nation. That's another aspect of the violence that we are experiencing. Recently, the tone of our talk seems to have worsened. Many words have been "coloured" by the kind of talk that would cause some groups in the society to stop talking to each other…to put it plainly.

So, if the talk elicits a response to hate or kill, then it's not acceptable. The Bible gives speech the highest rating in relations, and psychologists and sociologists would agree. What is said could cause grievous harm to others – words can cut like a knife. Just to say, even bad grammar would "harm" you. As my experienced journalist friend said to me the other day, "green verbs are painful to the ear"

But how can we really test the talk? There must be a yardstick to measure the intent and extent of words uttered.

So, it's time for the etymologists, linguists, and cultural conformists to come forward as experts, to set up a matrix, to ascertain when asinine statements are uttered. And if they are worth being weighed on the scales of good sense or jurisprudence. People should not be able to "get away" when they deliberately utter words that sicken the society.

No special freedoms and concessions must be given to people who seek to "murder with their mouths." In the old days, the use of "bad words" made parents want to wash out their children's mouths with soap.

Maybe we need some modern detergent as a deterrent for people with foul mouths, who think they are free to attack others with impudence.

The laws of Trinidad and Tobago include the obscene language/profanity laws which consider provocation and "breach of peace, or to the annoyance of any resident or person in [public] use of obscene or 'foul language' as a criminal act." Notably, there is a fine of $200 or imprisonment for 30 days. Not much of a deterrent.

Many consider the law to be oppressive, but we need to give serious consideration when such speech "can be oppressive to incite or has the potential to incite violence," according to our Constitution.

Wicked words must be expunged from our vocabularies. What we need is a comprehensive published list of "bad words" to measure malicious intent. Even the internet giant Google has a listing of 1,730 words that it considers abusive. But such words are different in each country. We should have our own set of Trini words to be tested.

But Creole cultural norms be damned. We cannot hide behind idioms and ole talk to cowardly hurt others, brandishing wicked words like cutlasses in the midday sun. The instances of verbal violence have gone deep in the psyche of our people and our leaders must not be allowed to escape with the ambiguity of meanings when they speak.

I recently learned that a group of scientists from the International Journal of Advance Scientific Research and Engineering Trends in India (Akanksha Gajbahar et al) proposed a paper titled "A method for abusive words detection using machine learning framework." That's a real consideration for the academics. But very damning words must be tested.

There should be added penalties of expulsion for abusive words in Parliament, where the bruising dialogue tends to exploit parliamentary privileges and the sensibilities of others. But if our leaders cannot get away with vile utterances in the House, they should not be able to escape unscathed in the public domain. It's time to "lock them up," Madam Speaker!

So, this is where we reach in the land of free speech when people take the liberty to poison our minds with words that divide us and distort the vision of our destiny. Sadly, our children hear and take to heart the divisive talk that tears us apart.

It must be made clear to all that if we abuse, we all lose, especially with words of hate or discord. So, let's have more common sense in our utterances and save ourselves, our children, and our nation from decadence.

COMMENTARY

DEMOCRACY IN DISTRESS

NEWSDAY

Wednesday, 13th July 2022

THE ONGOING saga in the United States regarding the Capitol Building riot on January 6, 2021, is of noteworthy consideration and relevance to us in TT. The episode directly threatens the preservation of democracy in that nation, the region, and the world. The situation was heightened by the role of the former president, relating to the actions of people known and unknown.

The matter is under investigation, with a House of Representatives committee convening its seventh hearing on Tuesday. I have taken a glance or two at the proceedings, but what we need to carefully observe is how the US government, the mighty defender of democracy, is contending with a violation of its own trust.

Given all that has transpired, it is obvious that democracy is in distress. Is it fatal? It's hard to tell. But the prognosis does not look good for those in the middle of the melee. It's a real bacchanal in the Washington capital, the centre of the democratic world.

It's indeed a testing time for that proven form of government and its threatened demise by the unwise.

There is a direct relationship between what is happening in the big US and little TT. We are both custodians of democracy, committed to the preservation of the freedoms we hold so dear; the rights to free press and expression enshrined in our constitution. But these must not be violated or trampled upon by perpetrators of civil disorder that put our people and our polity in jeopardy.

The well-known quote reminds us, "If your neighbour's house is on fire, wet yours." There is therefore a legitimate cause for concern, given the volatile political situation in the US.

But really, who would have thought that a sitting president would have been embroiled in such an episode? Such acts are usually left to the dictators in backward "shi———-" countries as he, President Donald Trump, was quoted as saying in the media.

Consequentially, the attack on the US Capitol unfolded like a Hollywood movie script, with a leading star, supporting actors and hundreds of extras storming the set. The Capitol Building was full of drama and intrigue, for all the world to see, but the full story is yet to be told.

Shortly after the fiasco, many saw the inauguration of President Joe Biden on the American "throne" as palliative care for a democracy in distress. But the question is still in the air: how well is the US democracy coping? We must be patient and prudent in our consideration that the concept and philosophy of democracy is being tested and may be falling apart as it seems.

In our deliberations, we must admit that we have been "supporting" the US democracy in taste, values and in dress, even as we strive to retain our own culture. We are branded forever. We are a nation born again to a Republican state, but our navel string is still tied to the foreign mother. The economic midwives still shape our lives.

The connection is deep. Over time, we have moved along, with many humming the melody to the familiar words of the US national anthem, "Oh say can you see..." And sending our children to be nurtured by the prudence of the North American political economy and culture. We are awash with American paraphernalia since the Chaguaramas base in the war days of the 1940s, spouting paranoia for things that totally belong to the American way.

No one can deny that the very air we breathe has the "fragrance" of the North American ideology. Our vision and habits have been patterned and "permatised." We are plagued by the myopic perception that we are free. But while the eagle seems to shape our destiny, we must never neglect to look for the corbeaux around in protecting our democracy from decay.

And so, the US, the cradle of western civilisation, seems to have taken a turn for the worse. The stage is set for the demise of the great nation if there is no turning or reconciliation in the contentions of its many professed positions on life, and all that we also consider dear. America needs to hear.

The concept of democracy that the US shares with TT has been shaken by the recent incidents and the presidential impeachments. We are in the midst of it. We can't escape the irony of the dependency on North American thinking. If that boat is sinking, so are we.

Even so, the same concept of theocracy that was the foundation of US democracy should remain central to any consideration for the resolution of issues. No state should drift away from its moorings, despite riots and other contentious issues. The teaching of the "God in whom we can trust" should continue to be the core concept for democratic freedom in any nation.

What then is the destiny of TT's democracy? We have our own share of distress. But we must maintain integrity in our democracy. We must watch out for the crazy talk and nefarious actions that are creating cracks and crevices in our form of government. The issue of corruption is choking us, and we don't seem to have the constitution to withstand the onslaught. We are tripping over each other in our attempts at putting things right, but all too often in a wrong way.

We must strive to preserve our place in the sun. Our nationalism has been an infusive force in the pathway of our progress; we must preserve our democracy by any means necessary. What has been going on in the US must never happen to us. We must put laws in place to stop any creeping dictatorship or the scourge of race in party politics. We must ensure accountability in parliamentary representation and demand honesty from those in high offices. That is the burden of our democracy.

So, while we sit in the pavilions of life and view the strife amidst the US leadership, we must see it all, not merely as a march to the Capitol, but a march in time to eternity. That is our true manifest destiny.

The US and TT share a common philosophy of democracy, but we must both continue to embrace theocracy. With that philosophy, there is a clear destination. There is a God, and we must change our alliance from a reliance on the North American ideal to a model of governance with its focus fully on the divine. And never forget that the one who truly rules the affairs of man is not of this land or any other.

So, what about the ongoing drama in the Capitol in Washington? The saga continues like a sequel from a movie thriller, but in real-time. We watch and pray; we look and learn.

Our eyes are on North America, but our hearts must belong to God.

STOP HATING OUR HERITAGE

Note: Sent for publication. No access to the Archives)

The hatred of our heritage is a strong deterrent to our progress as a nation. It is evidenced in the way we treat our environment, our monuments, and the relics of the past. We have bastardized our historical legacy and the natural and built heritage of our beautiful country. It seems like we love to hate our own.

In recent times, we have seen several historic buildings torn down with disdain, in Sangre Grande, Port of Spain, San Fernando and even Mayaro, all relegated to the dust, in the name of progress. In the process, we have literally dumped our heritage like the litter scattered over our countryside.

Many of our beautiful antique edifices, vandalized and abandoned, our historic landscapes ravaged, like an act of war. We are denying the future for our children, by failing to preserve the past and protect the present, for the sake of the future. We are killing our heritage.

We seem resigned to benefit from the solo efforts of a few passionate people, a few political pronouncements and the promises of prioritization of token efforts to preserve our heritage. But all seem limited or lacking in completeness.

Meanwhile, our institutions tasked with preserving our heritage are afforded limited resources and even less legal latitude to champion our many heritage projects. We credit their patriotic efforts.

Over the years, the support for heritage preservation has been transient from the powers that be; lip service and plenty of platitudes have been the norm. Much has been said, but very little has been done to protect and preserve our heritage.

And again, another building goes, callously, carelessly... we move on after a day or two of protest, whispering and whimpering in the corners of our homes. And concerned custodians stand helplessly by, unable to save the day or to rescue the situation.

Arguments, explanations, and excuses have tumbled upon each other, blocking the doorway to hope of preservation or restoration efforts, as the years pass, and our heritage fades away.

As a nation, we need to see what we have been, in order to shape what we must become. It is sad when we pontificate and postulate on issues of national development and pat ourselves on our backs at our annual awards, while we deny and destroy the very things that are essential to our success, as a third-world-becoming-first-world-nation.

Our heritage is our legacy. It is a sacred responsibility. Our efforts today must not be scurried by the vagaries of economics or the wanton disregard for values and national pride. We must skip over the persistent obstacles of race and politics and other tricks, to create a country that is serious about its place in history, and one that does not neglect the very heritage that defines it.

While I credit the efforts of the pioneers, there is the need to raise awareness, commitment, and demonstration of a passion for our place in the world. Our heritage must live on in the hearts of every primary school child and in the corridors of power and on the silent hills of our countryside. We are compelled to do what must be done to save our heritage. Our preservation efforts must become as commonplace as our willingness to lime and fete. 'We eh reach there yet.'

Today, I call for a concerted patriotic effort by all, to save our heritage. We need to martial our forces along the tracks and trails and along the busy causeways of our country. There are many stories to be told, and places to preserve about the Indigenous people, oil and gas, the railway days, the sugarcane chapter, the churches, and other institutions.

How easily we engage in dialogue and wander into a diatribe of the current bacchanal, preoccupied with the things that rise like chaff to the wind, while the evidence of our existence remains neglected and rotting away, covered with the vines of time, forgotten and forlorn.

We must do something to save our heritage. Each child must be taught to truly appreciate our culture and heritage. Make the teaching of our history mandatory and immediate, make the preservation of old buildings a legal requirement, make the promotion of our heritage a priority in our regional corporations and institutions, and make corporate companies accountable for preserving our natural and built heritage.

But then, some erstwhile person will say that those measures are already in place. Then I say, in the face of such a declaration... don't just tell me, show me that we really love our heritage.

"The lines have fallen to me in pleasant places; indeed, my heritage is beautiful to me. The Bible (Psalm 16:5b.)

APOSTLE TERRENCE HONORÉ
PALMISTE SAN FERNANDO

Apostle Terrence Paul Honoré is a bold commentator on issues that affect the church and the society. He is an ordained minister of religion. This publication is in celebration of his 50th year in ministry, having started his preaching career back in 1972.

He is an accomplished journalist having worked as a writer for the Texaco Star (International Publication), the Trintoc News and the Petrotrin Newsletter for a total of 15 years. He completed a 4-year Certificate in Mass Communication at the University of the West Indies with majors in Radio & TV and Journalism back in 1982. He won the top award for 'Contemporary Issues' in the Final year.

Apostle Honoré completed his degree in History and Social Sciences at UWI on a Trintoc Scholarship and followed with a Certificate in Quality Management, UWI/Institute of Business. He is recognized for preparing cohesive professional documents, position papers etc that have been used in secular and Christian circles.

He served for 33 years in the oil industry in the Instrument Department, the Public Relations Department and the Human Resources Unit, before moving to administration in the Medical Department. He took up a position as Hospital Management in the public health industry. He lectured for five years on Communications and Public Relations with the UWI Continuing Studies.

Apostle Honoré has used his experience in journalism to advance his Christian worldview. He has written dozens of letters to the editors of the local newspapers from 1994 to present. A selection of these articles is presented in this publication.

He serves as the Founder and President of the Christian Historical Society and sees this, publication as an apostolic view of what has transpired over the period under review. He considers this a historical document, as much as it is a commentary on contemporary issues. He continues to write letters to the editor till the present time.

THANK YOU

I wish to acknowledge the management of the Trinidad and Tobago NEWSDAY newspaper and the Trinidad Guardian, for publishing most of the letters I sent to the Editor. Thank you for providing such a wonderful forum for expression.

www.ingramcontent.com/pod-product-compliance
Lightning Source LLC
LaVergne TN
LVHW041711070526
838199LV00045B/1295